a Gift for ne
Mo

a Gift for new Mothers

Traditional Wisdom of Pregnancy, Birth and Motherhood

DEBORAH JACKSON

dbp

DUNCAN BAIRD PUBLISHERS

LONDON

A Gift for New Mothers
Deborah Jackson

This paperback edition published in the United Kingdom and Ireland in 2005 by
Duncan Baird Publishers
Sixth Floor, Castle House
75–76 Wells Street
London W1T 3QH

Conceived, created and designed
by Duncan Baird Publishers

First published in Great Britain as Eve's Wisdom (hardback) in 1999
and as Mother & Child (paperback) in 2002 by
Duncan Baird Publishers

Project Editor: Kirsten Chapman
Editor: Zoë Fargher
Managing Designer: Dan Sturges
Designer: Rebecca Johns
Commissioned artwork: Jamie Bennett, Fabian Negrin, Leigh Wells

British Library Cataloguing-in-Publication Data:
A catalogue record for this book is available from the British Library.

1 3 5 7 9 10 8 6 4 2

ISBN: 1-84483-128-0

Typeset in GillSans and MrsEaves
Colour reproduction by Colourscan, Singapore
Printed by Imago, Thailand

PUBLISHER'S NOTES
The abbreviations BCE and CE have been used in this book:
BCE Before the Common Era (equivalent to BC)
CE The Common Era (equivalent to AD)

The Publisher and author recommend that medical advice is sought before attempting any of the exercises or herbal or other treatments suggested in this book. They can take no responsibility for any injury, damage or other adverse effect resulting from following any of the suggestions herein.

In order to avoid any gender bias, "he" and "she" are used
interchangeably in this book to refer to a baby.

Contents

Introduction

The future of mothering is a cause for concern in the West. Ancient assumptions about maternal instinct and infant bonding are being eroded by scientists, who inform us that the natural emotions of motherhood are little more than a series of chemical reactions and physical cues. It seems there's no magic about mothers any more.

After giving birth a Western mother is often under pressure to return to "real" work. Staying at home to look after her baby is often considered to be simply domestic dawdling, a second-class role that could be undertaken by anyone. Many women feel torn between conflicting roles if they attempt to be both caring mothers and effective working professionals.

In many parts of the world, despite advances in science and communication, there are women who are untouched by these debates and conflicts. They fulfil a legacy of motherhood that has been handed down for generations. In places where the most urgent purpose is survival, mothers themselves are recognized as the guardians of life. Parenthood is an elevated role, surrounded with mystery and wonder; celebrated with feasts and rituals; protected with taboos.

This book is not an uncritical celebration of all things ethnic. Instead, it gathers together a diverse range of insights into the universal subjects of bearing and raising children, from the world's rich source of practical wisdom. And as we celebrate our differences, we may once again feel connected in our common task of raising the children and parents of the future.

CHAPTER 1

The Time of Promise

Enclosed in his cocoon, the unborn child is a source of joy and anticipation. He teases his mother with fluttering movements and entertains her with dreams rich in symbols. The nine months of waiting are a chance to prepare body and mind for the completely new focus of motherhood. As you eat, breathe and move, you do so on another's behalf.

The Mother Goddess

Every one of us was carried for nine months – or thereabouts – in the all-embracing comfort of our mother's womb. This simple, universal fact of life probably formed the basis of humanity's earliest religions.

Prehistoric peoples were in awe of the Great Mother, a divine figure from whom all life flowed. Many scholars believe that this female deity of life and fertility may have been the sole object of devotion for our early ancestors. The theory is that, long before complex civilizations emerged with their ranks of household gods, and before the arrival of an all-powerful masculine godhead, there was only one being considered worthy of adoration: the all-giving mother goddess.

Traditions of the divine mother figure throughout the world tell of her life-giving powers. Aditya, the ancient Iranian goddess who represented vast primordial space, gave birth to seven children, who became the gods of the sun, moon and stars. Bachue, a mother goddess of the

Incas, gave birth to the first humans before transforming herself into a snake and returning to the sacred waters of the lake from which she had first emerged.

In Greek mythology the earth mother Gaia conceived by herself and gave birth to the sky-god Uranus. The subsequent union of the two gods produced huge monsters with a hundred hands, three Cyclopes, and the first generation of Greek gods (six ferocious Titans and six formidable Titanesses).

The match between earth mothers and sky fathers is repeated in many ancient religions. In the Maori creation myth, Papa, the earth mother, and Rangi, the sky father, were clasped in an eternal embrace. They held each other so tightly that their unborn children, the gods of nature, were imprisoned in Papa's womb. Tane, the future god of the forests, decided to separate Rangi and Papa. From within the womb he raised his father sky with his head and pushed his mother earth downward with his feet. The embrace was released and the gods of nature were born.

In Chinese myth, the goddess Nu Wa created the first humans from mud, but the task became too great for her: "I can't make mud dolls for ever. Have families and fill the world!"

Ancient goddesses may have been infinitely fertile – benign archetypes with open arms and ample, childbearing hips – but the Great Mother also had darker incarnations. The Morrigan, a terrifying Celtic goddess in triple form, controlled death and sexuality as well as the forces of life. Her flame-haired figure was sometimes depicted with three heads or even three bodies. In other accounts the Morrigan was known as Badhbh, meaning "boiling", and was symbolized by a bubbling cauldron which disgorged all life.

Mother goddesses presided over the thresholds of human experience, guiding babies into existence and shepherding the dying toward the afterlife. They were the objects of both awe and fear, and were often invoked as the final arbiters over the survival of a newly delivered baby or of safely gathered crops. In the Balkans people still make corn dollies, representing the ancient goddess Nerthus, to ensure a plentiful harvest.

In ancient Rome Juno (consort and sister of the great god Jupiter) was the guardian of women and childbirth – the equivalent of the Greek deity Hera. While Jupiter was god of the sky and bringer-of-light, Juno was the goddess of the moon and the guardian of all things dark, hidden and female. For the ancient Romans a woman's *juno*, or protective female spirit, would guide her as she entered a new home, increase her fertility and assist her during pregnancy and labour. It was believed that Juno bestowed the gift of sight on newborn babies.

When the Romans conquered Britain, aspects of the popular Celtic goddess Brigit, protector of women and childbirth, were assimilated into Juno, including the title Queen of Heaven. Brigit was Christianized and regarded as the midwife or foster-mother of Jesus. According to a Hebridean Christian fable, Brigit placed three drops of pure water on the holy infant's brow. This belief was adapted from an older pagan story in which the goddess Brigit bestowed a blessing of triple

purity (three drops of wisdom) on the Son of Light. Scottish Highlanders in the Hebrides used to offer their prayers for safe childbirth to Brigit "the Bride".

Ajysyt, Great Mother to the Siberian Yakut tribe, lived in heaven, writing down the fate of each child in a golden book. She watched over every baby's birth and brought a soul from heaven to complete the newborn child.

Meskhenet, an Egyptian goddess who presided over childbirth, acted as sacred midwife and was believed to arrange each baby's destiny. Mothers would offer prayers for a healthy baby to Meskhenet, whose symbol was the birthing tile over which mothers squatted in labour.

Today mother goddess cults have virtually vanished in the West, but women can rediscover their symbolic power by celebrating their divine foremothers. You could commemorate Yule (December 21), the winter solstice, when mother goddesses such as the Babylonian Ishtar and Astarte traditionally gave birth to the sun. You might observe the Celtic festival of Imbolc – literally "in the womb" – on February 1, to revere the heavily pregnant mother earth. On May Night you could mark Celtic Beltane (May 1), when the May Queen married the sun god to restore universal harmony, after the upheaval of winter decay and spring regeneration.

EARTH AND WATER

Over 2,500 years ago the ancient Greeks believed that four elements were essential to human life: air and fire were male, earth and water female. Earth was the key element: the source of shelter and food for all living things.

To our early ancestors mountains were embodiments of mother goddesses and mountain caves were the wombs of creation. Childless earth-worshipping women pressed themselves to the ground, in the hope of becoming fertile. Ancient Roman women placed their newborn babies on the ground in a gesture of thanks to the life-giving earth. Even today caves and rock formations in the shape of the *yoni* (sacred vulva) are worshipped in India.

Water is linked with fecundity and birth. Early ancestors of the Finns and Hungarians prayed to a Water Mother for babies; while African women traditionally gave birth near rivers and streams, drawing strength from the sound of the rushing water.

Water also symbolizes rebirth: rain regenerates dry soil; baptism marks the beginning of new life; flood myths, found in many cultures, represent a chance to start afresh; trickling water promises rejuvenation and growth.

The female elements can provide spiritual sustenance during pregnancy. Try walking barefoot in a garden – imagine yourself connecting with mother earth as you do so. Or sit by a river or stream, close your eyes and listen to the sound that the water makes. Visualize the course of pregnancy as the current of a flowing river.

Mother Earth, Father Sky

Weave us clothing of great brightness

That we may walk where birds sing and grass grows green.

Oh, our mother the earth,

Oh, our father the sky.

PRAYER OF THE TEURA PEOPLES OF NEW MEXICO

Conceiving is Believing

The medical explanation for the miracle of life often seems inadequate. *Where do babies come from*? is a universal question that has been explained in a huge variety of ways, from euphemisms of baby-producing gooseberry bushes and benevolent storks in the West, to cyclical Buddhist journeys of reincarnated spirits in the East.

In many cultures conception is more than a biological event – it is a spiritual interaction. Ainu children in Japan are regarded as the physical embodiments of their ancestors' spirits. In Thailand conception is regarded as the moment when a soul enters a woman's body during intercourse. This soul will have lived many times before and its character will be fully formed. However, the rebirth indicates that it has not yet attained the highest level of disembodied spiritual existence.

For some tribal peoples sex is not considered necessary for conception. Anbarra Aborigines in central Arnhem Land, Australia, say that "spirit children" were placed in

certain freshwater pools and water holes during the Dreamtime. Women who want to conceive visit areas rumoured to be rich in spirit babies. These beings are rarely seen, for they are said to be as small as walnuts. Each spirit child chooses a mother who it thinks will be kind, swims inside her, and in this way she becomes pregnant. Another widespread Aboriginal conception belief is that if a man traps a spirit child in the form of a fish or an animal while hunting and then feeds it to his wife, she will conceive. The child will have certain attributes of the animal's spirit, and even a physical mark in the same place that the animal was speared by the father.

In old England sowing parsley was said to bring babies. When children asked where they came from, they were often told that they came out of the parsley bed.

According to the Dogon people of West Africa, for conception to occur a man must whisper tales of the ancient ancestors into a woman's ear before lovemaking. The words then swirl down to the womb to become the celestial liquid impregnated by the man's essence.

The Greek philosopher Aristotle believed that semen was the sole source of life, but in some societies the father is regarded as superfluous to conception. Women of the Kayapó tribe of Brazil conduct their own impregnation rituals deep in the forest. Standing in a river, stripped to the waist, the woman is brushed with leaves by her friends; they tie a vine around her waist and she drinks special bark juice. Although they realize where babies come from, the women attain a certain amount of sexual freedom through this ritual – women who don't wish to be restricted to one husband say that they are expecting a forest baby, a gift from Mother Nature herself.

A SEA-VOYAGE BACK TO LIFE

The Trobriand Islanders of the South Pacific have one of the most enchanting conception beliefs in the world. Each newborn child is said to be a rejuvenated spirit who has chosen to journey back to life, across the sea, from the Island of the Dead. The spirit floats back to the islands, clinging to driftwood and sacred seaweed to ease his journey, and a woman conceives by bathing in the ocean and "catching" one of the spirits. The returning spirit itself has no name, but it is believed to rejoin the mother-line of its previous birth.

Fishermen claimed to hear the spirits crying "wa wa" over the waves and, even today, the Trobriand Islanders' word for "fetus" is *waiwaia*, a continual reminder of the spiritual journey of all babies.

Mysteries of Gender

If a Jamaican woman sees shoals of fish swimming through her dreams, she takes it as a sign that a baby is probably on the way – but still the question remains, will the baby be a boy or girl? All over the world people look for signs of the baby's sex. If we believe gender myths, the baby's sex can be determined at any time during pregnancy – and even before it.

Gender speculation has grown up mostly because many cultures had an inevitable curiosity about the unborn child. The widespread belief that the continuation of the male line was paramount may have encouraged people to try to discover the gender of their baby.

In Hungary, eastern Europe, it is believed that, if a pregnant woman wishes to bear a son, she should place seeds from a poppy on the window sill of her home. If she would prefer to have a girl, she must sprinkle sugar grains there instead.

The Greek philosopher Aristotle promoted the belief that a man's right testicle produced boys while his left created girls. Thus, men in Ancient Greece who wanted sons often had their left testicle tied up and, in some very extreme cases, removed.

In ancient Mexico it was believed that the "nature essence" of either the mother or father would determine the child's sex during intercourse. As the parents made love, the mouth of the uterus was said to open and a drop of blood would fall into it from either parent. If the first drop was the mother's blood, the baby would be a boy; if the father's, a girl would be born. For the Zulus of southern Africa, if a green or black snake appears in the homestead, the newborn will be a boy, while a puff-adder signifies a girl.

Many gender divination techniques focus on the mother's actions, or what happens to her during pregnancy. In some cultures it is believed that the baby's sex can be both determined and influenced at this time – if the mother-to-be behaves in a certain way she can encourage nature to bring her a boy or a girl as is her wish. The mother's appearance is also supposed to give clues to the gender of the baby. The ancient Greek physician Hippocrates believed that the left eye and left breast were bigger in a woman who was expecting a baby girl – the opposite, of course, for a baby boy. Native North Americans looked for tiny fish-hook symbols in the whites of a woman's eyes beneath her irises. Fish-hook shapes in the right eye were said to signify a girl; in the left, a boy. (If hooks appeared in both eyes it was said that the woman was expecting twins, or simply that she already had children.)

In England women today follow an old-wives' tale that boys are carried in front, and girls are carried around the sides and front, wrapping themselves close to their mothers for protection.

Among the Dusin of northern Borneo, parents-to-be believe that a boy fetus moves quickly and roughly, while a girl moves quietly and gently. The Hamar people of southern Ethiopia believe that whenever Barjo, or Fate, creates a new human being, if the child smiles at the moment of birth, she becomes a woman.

If you are curious to test a prediction device, try an ever-popular test that originated among the Romany people. This method of gender speculation is still practised throughout the whole of Europe. Prop yourself up on cushions, so that you feel comfortable. Lie back so that your stomach (and the baby) face skyward. Ask a member of your family or a close friend to tie a pure gold ring (your wedding ring if you have one) onto a length of string or cotton, and hold it suspended above your stomach. The ring should start to move. A strong, circular movement is said to indicate that you are carrying a girl; a swing from side to side, like the movement of a pendulum, is said to mean a boy.

Of course, it makes no difference what the signs and portents are, as the gender of a baby is determined from the moment the sperm meets the egg and is beyond our control. Our role is not to change our developing baby, but to welcome and cherish whoever he or she may turn out to be.

DREAM BABIES

In cultures where a child's sex may be of great importance to the expectant parents, the symbols in a pregnant woman's dreams may be closely examined for gender clues. Across many diverse cultures dream gender symbols fall into two categories: round objects symbolize a female child and long, phallic-shaped objects are thought to suggest that a male child is on the way.

Nyinba women of Nepal suspect that they are carrying a boy if they dream of long vegetables, such as aubergines. (They also say that cutting tools, traditionally male implements, indicate a boy.) Alternatively they say that "girl" dreams feature round vegetables, as well as prayer beads and other circular objects.

In modern societies in the West, a child's sex may not be a matter of great importance to the parents. However, pregnancy dreams can still be interpreted as indicators of a mother's hopes and expectations for her future child. For example, it is common to dream of a baby who is imperfect in some way. Presenting this possibility in your dreams is your mind's way of preparing you for some of the uncontrollable aspects of motherhood.

Try writing a dream diary during pregnancy. See if you can interpret your dream images in the context of your waking life. Over time your own personal patterns of dream symbolism, and your unspoken feelings about your child, will emerge.

Movement and Meditation

You can prepare your body for the physical task of labour by taking regular exercise during pregnancy, although always consult your doctor before you begin any physical activity. Swimming is usually ideal during pregnancy as your body (and your unborn baby) is supported by the water. Although it might seem strange, belly dancing can help to prepare the pelvis and abdominal muscles for birth.

Yoga's Tailor Pose helps to soften ligaments during pregnancy. After a warm bath, sit on the floor with your back straight and bring the soles of your feet together in front of you. Breathing deeply, slowly draw your feet toward your body. With each out-breath, relax the hips and spine. Allow your knees to open out toward the floor.

WITH BABIES IN MIND

"Think beautiful thoughts" is an age-old prescription for pregnancy, but not always easy in a busy world. Take time out, as pregnant women in China and Japan used to do, for a daily meditation with your baby – a simple and beneficial way to begin the subtle bonding process.

Sit comfortably and slow your breathing. You could try a Zulu pregnancy breathing exercise before beginning to meditate: take three consecutive in-breaths so that your lungs are filled with air, and then one long out-breath to expel negative thoughts (visualize them disappearing) and energize your body. Imagine your baby and sense her, small, warm and protected, in the amniotic fluid. Spend a few minutes in open awareness. When you become skilled at harnessing your mind's energies, you can use them later to ease birth.

Visualize a place where you can be happy and alone – a garden, for example. Look around you and enjoy the tranquillity. When you are ready, walk further into your picture, perhaps into a secluded courtyard, where water trickles and birds sing. Affirm the positive messages you will need to hear during labour: your body opens easily, each contraction bringing your baby closer. Finally, turn and walk up the steps, through your garden and back into the moment. Practise finding your inner refuge in this way throughout pregnancy, perhaps using a physical trigger, such as clasping your hands.

A Sensory Connection

Some people say that a new baby cannot feel pain. But still, even in the womb his senses are highly alert. For example, his ears are adjusted so that through the amniotic fluid he is able to hear his mother's heartbeat and some of the sounds from outside her body, modulated by a liquid world.

Sensory perception is highly developed in the womb. A baby's skin, so smooth and sensitive, is

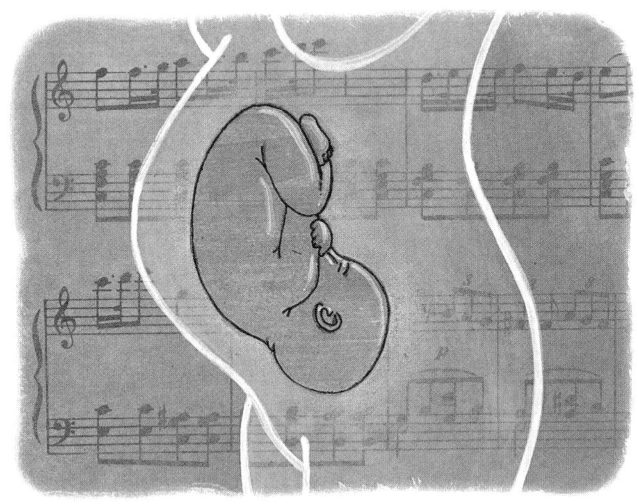

protected by fine hair and a layer of grease (vernix). Babies also have a wonderful capacity for taste, with tastebuds all over the mouth and tongue, tens of thousands more than they will have when they are ten years old.

The sense that most closely connects the unborn baby with the outside world is his ability to hear. As the mother talks to her child, she imprints herself on his brain, making a pre-natal bond that will continue throughout his life. In the Congo a pregnant woman sings to her unborn baby. The same song is repeated over and over throughout pregnancy to allow the child to associate the sound with security and comfort. Then, after the birth, the mother sings the song to her baby again. The familiar sound is immediately comforting to the child, who is calmed by the way in which it resonates through the bombardment of mysterious and bewildering sounds in his new world outside the womb.

Balinese babies are held constantly for their first 105 days, as the physical contact reminds them of the womb and helps to make them feel safe in their new environment

HAPPINESS OUTSIDE AND IN

Some people believe that, just as sounds can filter from the outside world into the womb and be heard by the unborn baby, emotions and thoughts can be transferred, too.

In Thailand an unborn child is thought to react to all the stimuli that affect his mother. As a result, she takes great care to have only positive experiences during her pregnancy. A pregnant Thai woman is also careful never to watch another woman giving birth. It is believed that, through his mother's eyes, the baby being born would be embarrassed to be "watched" by another baby, and that the baby "watching" would be embarrassed by what he sees. As a consequence, both babies would refuse to be born easily.

Elsewhere some mothers put pressure on their families and their friends to improve their behaviour so that the unborn child learns only good and decent human actions, which he will then take into his own life.

The idea that a mother's happiness influences her unborn baby is related in an ancient story that blends Christian and pagan traditions. Before Christ was born Mary and Joseph visited a cherry orchard. Mary asked her husband to pick her a cherry, but Joseph refused. Mary became sad and this melancholy was sensed by the unborn Christ who, desiring his mother's happiness, bade the tree bow down its branches to offer fruit to her. Thus Mary's happiness, and that of her baby, were restored.

Calming the Waves

Pregnancy is supposed to be a time when women "bloom" into visions of radiant beauty. Many mothers-to-be exude health and happiness, especially in the middle months, but there may well be times when you feel more like wilting.

Waves of tiredness and nausea can be the first signs of pregnancy; in countries where tests are

unavailable, women welcome these symptoms as proof that they are truly pregnant.

Nevertheless, every culture has its own preferred remedy for "morning sickness". In Indonesia women drink the juice of a young coconut. If the sickness is very severe, a midwife uses prayers and incantations to give the juice supernatural healing powers. In Austria mothers drink cups of fennel tea, while in Japan they eat the flesh of an umeboshi plum.

In ancient Rome pregnant women started the day with a drink of water infused with cinnamon and lime juice. Other nausea-calming teas include ginger (grate one teaspoon of fresh ginger root into a cup of hot water and let it steep for five minutes). A few drops of chamomile flower essence in water is an all-round pregnancy pick-me-up, easing nausea and stomach upsets, calming emotions and inducing restful sleep. Early nights and healthy snacks also help.

The ancient Egyptians pioneered the use of herbal medicine and essential oils, some of which are still used in the West today. However, you must seek advice from your doctor before you try these, as certain oils, such as sage and myrrh, should never be used while you are pregnant. During pregnancy your skin needs extra care – after all, it has to stretch to accommodate your growing baby.

Although stretch marks may appear, by caring for your skin during pregnancy you can help to reduce the tell-tale signs. Massage your skin with a mixture of 3 drops each of wheatgerm, borage seed and carrot oils in 50ml of almond oil. A wonderful evening massage mixture is 20 drops of lavender oil (a good sleep-aid) and 3 drops of neroli in 50ml of almond oil. Using light, sweeping movements, gently rub the oils into your skin. Massage your skin often during pregnancy and for a few months after birth. In traditional societies pregnant women meet their midwives for a tender massage with soothing preparations, from warm kukai oil in Hawaii to coconut oil in Malaysia. Cocoa butter is also widely used.

To help to prevent varicose veins, massage your legs with a mixture of 2 drops of geranium oil and 2 drops of lemon oil in 50ml of almond oil. Acupuncture, the ancient Chinese healing art which stimulates the release of energy blockages, can also be used to ease swollen veins or backache. Traditional remedies for heartburn (common in late pregnancy) include: peppermint tea; chewing almonds with orange peel; and the ancient Indian cure of a drop of sandalwood oil dissolved in honey water (taken before you go to bed).

FOOD FOR LIFE

A baby's organs are formed entirely during the first trimester, so it is clearly important for expectant mothers to eat well from conception. Your doctor will advise you on optimum pregnancy nutrition, but currently in vogue are oily fish (research from Denmark suggests that babies are born heavier), folic acid (from green, leafy vegetables) and even certain curries.

There is no single ideal diet but wholesome fresh food and a balance of nutrients are important. In the last trimester of pregnancy, some doctors recommend increased calcium and iron intake. Dairy products are excellent sources of calcium and green vegetables are rich in iron.

Stand under a mango tree and eat a mango. If you are expecting a baby, the fruit will taste like anything but a mango. This traditional pregnancy test from the Philippines reveals a fascinating feature of the antenatal state. Hormone production often makes the saliva taste metallic, which alters our sense of taste – even old favourites like coffee or tea may become unpalatable. Just as you may reject your favourite foods, you may also experience strange cravings. In Nepal, the Nyinba tribe believe that if a woman craves spicy food, she will have a girl; if she craves bland food, a boy is expected. Some women eat one unusual food to excess; others are drawn to comforting foods like porridge. A classic non-food craving is for coal, which can indicate mineral deficiency. Don't worry if you suddenly want a banana and onion pizza – your body is literally catering to its needs.

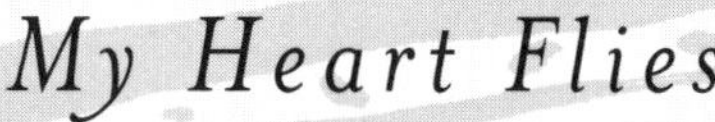

My Heart Flies

My heart is so joyous,
My heart flies in singing.
Under the trees of the forest,
The forest, our home, our mother.
In my net I have caught
A little bird,
A very little bird,
And my heart is caught
In the net with the little bird.

PREGNANCY SONG OF THE EFÉ PEOPLES

Seven-Month Ceremonies

At seven months an unborn child is almost fully formed in the womb, with eyelashes and her own unique fingerprints. She can swallow, suck her thumb, hiccup, hear sounds in the world beyond the womb, and even recognize her mother's voice. All over the world the seventh month of pregnancy is marked by ceremonies to rejoice in the new life unfurling.

Holding your own seven-month ceremony is a good way to celebrate your imminent motherhood and the growing vigour of your child. You might devise your own private "walkabout", introducing the child to favourite places or to the elements (represented by wind, sun, earth and water). In a ritual followed by the Quiché people of Guatemala, a mother describes the scene out loud to her unborn child (you could voice the words in your head if you prefer) and tells her about the woods, rivers and mountains.

You could even make your journey within the confines of your own home, taking the baby on a walk through the house, describing each room, what happens there and who spends time in it. You could introduce your baby to members of your family through photographs and share with her the relationships and memories that these represent.

Alternatively, you might consider making a symbolic commitment to the future. If it is autumn, for example, you might choose a special place in your garden and plant seven bulbs that will flower in the spring of your baby's arrival.

Feasting plays an important part in many seven-month rituals – most notably in Indonesia. The traditional Javanese feast takes place in the home of the maternal grandmother-to-be, emphasizing that the wisdom and experience of childbirth passes down through generations of women. The ceremonial table is laid with seven pyramids of rice to represent the seven months of pregnancy; eight or nine balls of rice to symbolize the saints who brought Islam to Indonesia; and another, larger rice pyramid, believed to give symbolic strength to the baby. In Indonesia

the child in the womb is thought of as a mystic meditating in a cave, strengthening herself spiritually for her emergence into the world.

In many ceremonies the guests perform symbolic tasks associated with the birth to come. The father, midwife, mother-in-law, friends all have parts to play; the ceremony marks the creation of the network of support that will guide the child through life. You could easily devise a ceremony of this kind to help to mark the turning-point before the more tiring, final months of pregnancy and the countdown to birth. In the box, right, are a few ideas that you may like to try or adapt for your own seven-month feast.

TIME FOR A FEAST

A pleasant feature of seven-month festivals is a meal to welcome friends and relatives into the company of your unborn child. Holding your own seven-month feast allows your loved ones to share your celebration. You could heighten the symbolism in various ways – for example, by hosting a dinner or lunch for seven people, perhaps asking each guest to bring along a dish. In the centre of the table you might set seven candles, perhaps held in a menorah – a sacred candelabrum, from Jewish tradition, with seven stems representing, among other things, the seven branches of the Tree of Life.

As a souvenir of the occasion, everyone, including yourself, could sign a special book, each person writing their own message to your child.

The Unfolding Lotus

Ripe fruit is plucked easily from a tree. But how do we know when a baby is ready to come? Contractions may begin in slow waves, as if the child is waking from a deep sleep. Waters breaking is a sure sign that labour is beginning.

In Malaysia midwives feel a woman's feet as she nears her time. When the big toe grows cold, it

means that body heat is shifting toward the womb, in preparation for labour.

Every culture has its own ways of preparing for labour and easing the baby's arrival. Thai women eat lotus buds blessed by a Buddhist monk, so their bodies will open like a lotus flower. According to Chakra (energy-centre) meditation, the crown of the head is a thousand-petalled lotus unfolding toward the divine energy of the universe. In labour, Indian women borrow this image, visualizing the cervix opening at each contraction.

Many birth treatments are suggestively slippery, symbolically willing the baby to slither out with ease. Before labour Cherokee mothers take a ritual bath infused with slippery bark; they also take a powerful herb to make the baby "jump down briskly". In the Yemen the midwife feeds the mother oil and milk.

Other treatments, such as perineal massage, are more practical. In the weeks leading up to birth, after a bath massage the area around the vagina with almond oil – add 5 drops of rose oil if you like. During labour a skilled midwife can give an internal massage before the baby has fully descended the birth canal.

Such natural methods may not involve technical wizardry, but births in "primitive" tribes are often fast and seemingly effortless.

CHAPTER 2

Into the World

World culture has developed myriad traditions to express the sacred significance of birth. Special consideration for the place of birth, an extraordinary diversity of methods for easing labour, rituals of thanksgiving and celestial birth charts all represent the culmination of nine months of passionate anticipation and express our profound hope for each precious new life.

Birthplace, Birthspace

Where is it best to give birth? For many women in the West, hospital is perceived as the safest place (particularly for a first birth), on account of its monitoring equipment and staff specially trained to spot and handle problems. But many women around the world

give birth safely outside a hospital environment. The simple answer may be: wherever you feel safe and happy.

Despite the proliferation of hospital birth centres, eight out of ten babies in the world are born at home. This may be in a special room, a space with spiritual and emotional meaning. Or it may be in the bedroom, often where the baby was actually conceived, and a place of obvious privacy.

In many parts of the world, women return to the home of their own mother in order to give birth, where they can be separate, safe and protected by those who know and love them best. Among the Basuto of Lesotho, a couple's first child actually "belongs" to the maternal grandparents and so is born in their house.

A common preparation for labour is the stopping up of holes and windows in the birthing room, which is said to keep out evil spirits. The effect is also to create a womb-like area, protected from prying eyes.

"She reclined, propped up with fair cushions of crimson damask with gold, and was wrapped about with a round mantle of crimson velvet furred with ermine."

AN ONLOOKER'S VIEW OF JANE SEYMOUR, QUEEN TO HENRY VIII OF ENGLAND, IN THE ROOM WHERE SHE GAVE BIRTH TO EDWARD VI

Most mothers seek seclusion, often in the familiarity of their own home, for this intimate act, but in some cultures birth was kept away from the home because the blood of childbirth was believed to pollute the household. Japanese women traditionally delivered their babies in small birthing sheds; in Smolensk births took place in a barn; and Arapesh women of New Guinea still give birth in special huts outside the village.

There are cultures in which childbirth is a major social event. When Navaho Native American mothers go into labour, the whole tribe gathers round to eat a meal and enjoy the spectacle. Among the Basque people of Spain, a mother in labour is traditionally attended by her whole family. Weather allowing, the birth takes place outside, near a running stream. There is singing, story-telling and jokes to "massage the mother and baby with laughter".

Yemenite women expect their neighbours and friends to visit during labour, to lend moral support, chant prayers to Allah and help out if necessary. In Yucatán Maya women in labour are not isolated from day-to-day life. They give birth in a blanket, slung from the rafters for

privacy, but this does not deter their friends from calling by to chat, or animals from wandering in and out. The calm atmosphere of normality helps to ease tension.

In places where childbirth was acknowledged as the most important and sacred human act, people designed their houses and villages with birth in mind. Extended Inuit families lived in a karmak, or semi-underground earth house, entered by a low, sloping passageway. As the karmak was symbolically associated with the womb, great care was taken to smooth the walls of the entrance, probably to ensure smooth births.

In medieval Europe noble women retreated to a designated

WATERS OF LIFE

Water is a universal birth aid, used directly for its soothing and cleansing properties and also as a birth stimulant. To soften the perineum African mothers labour over steaming hot rocks, and Guatemalan midwives give relaxing steam-bath massages.

Giving birth in water, which has become popular in the West, was rare until this century. During a modern waterbirth, immersion is used in the first stages of labour to relieve pain and to stimulate cervical dilation.

A newborn baby can survive underwater for up to forty minutes, so you can stay in the birthing tub to give birth. (Ensure that you consult your doctor about this.) As soon as the baby is born, he should be gently brought to the surface to take his first breath of air.

lying-in chamber for the weeks preceding and after birth. A noble woman would choose her own bed covers and drapes and the room would be equipped with an altar where Mass could be said. Only her husband, priest and ladies-in-waiting were permitted entrance.

Zulu women decorated the birth place with beads and carvings so that the newborn's eyes would fall immediately upon beautiful objects. Thai women festoon their houses with protective tokens – cloths painted with magical letters and pictures – to keep away the malevolent spirits that are said to gather around the birth room.

If you have planned where you will give birth, why not transform it into a personalized birthing domain? Inspirational pictures, such as those of happy family occasions, will help you with positive visualizations; an upstairs room with a view of the sky, rooftops or hills will give you a sense of space and freedom.

CATCHING BABIES

Birth is a bridge from one world to the next, and the mother and child making this journey can be vulnerable travellers. On every continent women turn to midwives to help them in labour.

A midwife's role does not always end with "catching babies", as Amish people call it. Traditional midwifery offers a continuous line of care, beginning before pregnancy and culminating with lifelong friendship. In Guatemala a *comadrona*, often a family friend, gives massage for period pains, works as a midwife and has long-term responsibility for the baby. She is part health-professional, part godmother – her concern extends to the spiritual as well as the medical.

Before it came to be treated as a medical condition, childbirth used to be a solely female concern. In English the word "midwife" is derived from the Anglo-Saxon phrase meaning simply "with woman".

This principle of female solidarity is illustrated by the Efé peoples in the rainforest of the Congo. At the onset of labour, two midwives accompany the mother to the river. They sing with her during the contractions and, as she squats at the water's edge, they support her on each side, breathing deeply. As the baby's head crowns, the midwives hold their breath and the baby is born. Jean-Pierre Hallet, a Belgian anthroplogist who, during the 1900s, lived with the Efé on and off for sixty years, described the birth occasion as a "tremendous feeling of oneness".

Goats Have No Midwives

Goats have no midwives,

Sheep have no midwives.

When the goat is pregnant, she is safely delivered,

When the sheep is pregnant, she is safely delivered,

You, in this state of pregnancy, will be safely delivered.

SONG OF THE AFRICAN YORUBA MIDWIFE

Easing the Way

Navaho Indians have two words to describe labour: one meaning "childbirth" and the other meaning "pain in labour". It is possible to have both, they say, but it is not necessary to have the second.

Many first-time mothers assume that childbirth will be painful. But using positive visualizations, such as imagining your body as a rose or lotus flower, or visiting your "safe place" (see box, page 26), combined with a supportive atmosphere, can ensure birth is a joyful experience.

According to the Cuna Indians of Panama, a goddess, Muu, lives in the womb. During a difficult birth she is said to have become too attached to the baby and a special chant is said to make her release the child.

In the seventeenth-century French women kept a lighted candle and a Resurrection Flower, or "Rose of Jericho", by their bedside during labour. This "rose" is actually a desert plant that forms a tight ball when dry and unfolds and blooms when moistened. According to Christian folklore the flower was said to

bloom at Christmas, close its petals on the anniversary of the Crucifixion and re-open them on the anniversary of the Resurrection. The unfolding flower is a symbolic reminder of the body opening for birth. The melting candle represents the progress of labour.

However, traditional birth aids are not always so poetic: the Rajputs (an Indian warrior caste) place a sickle, a knife and a ploughshare beneath the bed to "cut" the pain. During a difficult labour an African Ga midwife will give the mother a thorough brushing with a broom to chase away spirits.

Massage can be a wonderful birth tonic. In Bangladesh, massage by the *dai*, or midwife, is considered to be the best form of pain relief, as it provides constant physical and emotional support. During labour an Australian Aboriginal woman walks around, and leans against a tree. As birth approaches a female relative sits behind her and supports her back, while other women massage her abdomen "to help the baby to come down". To revive sluggish contractions ask your birth assistant to massage the tops and soles of your feet, applying particular pressure to your heel and ankle, which are acupressure points.

In the Philippines a midwife of the Bagos tribe performs the ritual of *kistat* – making as much noise as possible to force the baby out. In England the pealing of church bells was believed to help delivery – perhaps the background noise made mothers feel less inhibited

THIS WAY, THAT WAY, FORWARDS AND BACKWARDS

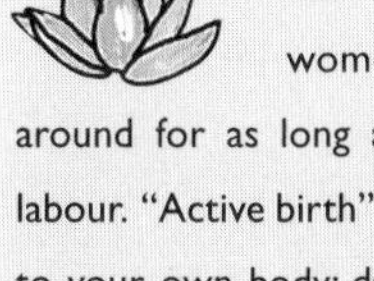

Take a tip from African women, who walk around for as long as possible during labour. "Active birth" means responding to your own body: dancing, leaning and crouching can all be part of your repertoire. When it comes to the moment of birth, each culture has its preferred position. You may be asked to lie on your back in a hospital, but in some tribes this position is taboo and thought to restrict the baby's blood supply. Zinacanteco women of Mexico crouch over a specially-woven reed mat; Sudanese women hang onto a rope suspended from the ceiling; African women often kneel in an upright position. A helpful recent addition to the birth kit is the bean bag, which adapts itself to any position you may choose.

about shouting out. You could help to banish your own inhibitions by preparing background music for birth. Experiment with a variety, to suit the changing emotions of labour. Gentle classical music or echoes of the sea can help you to focus in the early stages. African drumbeats and strong rhythms are wonderful at later active moments. Be sure to have some soft music ready to welcome your baby.

A SHARED EXPERIENCE

In the Yucatán the baby's father is expected to be present during labour to "see how a woman suffers". The ancient tradition of couvade (from the Latin word *cubare*, meaning to lie down) requires a father to sympathize even more directly, by mirroring the experience of the mother in late pregnancy and childbirth. Before the birth the husband takes to his bed and fasts or abstains from certain foods. During his wife's labour the husband groans in simulated pain. Couvade is still practised today in South America, Siberia, Africa and Malaysia. Ritual clothes-swapping is a less demanding way of sharing childbirth. In remote parts of southern India, men don their wives' saris during childbirth. Traditionally an Irish father gave symbolic strength to his wife in labour by giving her his waistcoat or watch to wear.

The Gift of a Lifetime

In English folklore butterflies were said to be the souls of babies who had not yet been named. The act of naming a child is believed to be a covenant that binds the newborn child to the real world – now he is no longer a stranger, but a member of a family and a wider community.

The time of naming varies greatly. In Christian cultures where a name was traditionally regarded as an important form of spiritual protection, naming ceremonies take place very soon after birth. However, in the Nicobar Islands in the Indian Ocean, names are given as a sign of independence and are only bestowed when a child begins to walk.

"A good name is better than precious ointment."

ECCLESIASTES 7:1

In many cultures a name is regarded as a significant gift to the child rather than as a means of identification: parental choices are replete with meaning, whether spiritual, social or shrewdly descriptive. For the Ibani of Nigeria, the name Bitegeriagha, "a cloth cannot

speak", expresses the inherent value of the child (cloth is the Ibani measure of wealth). Children are often named according to parents' hopes and expectations. A boy from Vietnam might be called Tuan Ahn, meaning Famous One. An Arab girl could be named Saideh (Lucky).

Possibly the most uninspired way to name a child is by order of birth, but in the days of large families this was not uncommon. Many boys in ancient Rome were called simply Primus, Secundus, Tertius (First, Second, Third). Balinese parents start with a number-name, but then elaborate it as they get to know the child. A fourth-born who was easily upset became Ketut Jangling – "fourth child who cries when he is put down".

There is often a generational cycle, with grandparents and babies sharing the same name. According to traditional Jewish custom, children are named after loved ones who have died, thus creating a name chain that can be traced right back through the family tree.

If you are having difficulty choosing the right name, try the Hawaiian method of dreaming the answer. Before sleeping meditate on your baby, and ask yourself to dream of a name. It might be spoken, or revealed symbolically for you to interpret: dreaming of a princess could imply the Hebrew name Sarah (which itself means "princess"). A dream about rocks or mountains might lead you to Peter, which is derived from the Greek word *petras*, meaning "rock", or Winston, which means "friendly rock".

A name given at birth is not always permanent. For example, the African name Masani, meaning "child who has a gap between the teeth" (a portent of good luck), is obviously given after teeth appear.

Welcome to the World

In celebrating birth we embrace the limitless possibilities of a new life. In nearly all cultures, traditions and rituals have emerged to offer thanks for a safe delivery and welcome the baby into the world.

Large meals, often involving the whole community, are a widespread way to welcome a new baby. You may prefer to have a private session of thanksgiving after birth, and a party for family and friends a few weeks later when you feel stronger.

In Brazil, a Tapirape father colours his hair with red dye from the annatto tree to announce the arrival of his newborn child.

After a traditional European christening ceremony, alcohol is consumed, often in copious quantities, to "wet the baby's head". In Holland the customary christening meal was very elaborate, with songs, speeches and a table laden with sugary delicacies. The *kandeel pot*, a tall goblet filled with sweetened Rhine wine, stood in the centre of the table and was stirred with a cinammon stick, which is long for a boy, but short for a girl.

The element of water has always been connected with birth rites. The Christian tradition of baptism is intended to cleanse the baby from sin, and anointing the baby's head with blessed water originated with the early Indo-Europeans and is still practised by Hindu priests in India. On the morning of a Russian Orthodox christening, three days after the birth, the family collects "holy water" from a nearby river and sprinkles it around the house.

The elements of fire and earth also play a part in traditional welcoming ceremonies. You could light a birth candle and pass the baby high over it, from mother to father, as is the custom in parts of Africa. In ancient Gaelic culture a new baby would "take a turn through the smoke" soon after birth to drive away the Hidden People who were believed to cause harm by touching or

singing to babies. The infant was handed across a candle flame three times, from midwife to father.

After the first weeks have passed, babies are often officially introduced to the outside world. A Guatemalan mother introduces her baby to nature when it is safe to take the child outside: she visits streams, volcanos and trees with her baby asking for their protection in the child's future. You could create a similar ritual: take your baby to a park and carry her beneath the trees, and quietly ask the trees for their protection.

PLANTING A BIRTH TREE

For early civilizations trees were the children who grew between Mother Earth and Father Sky, with their roots in the ground and their branches reaching heavenward. All over the world people plant trees to celebrate the new arrival.

In Germany fruit and nut trees are planted as symbolic companions for "the fruit of the womb" (the German word for fruit is *Obst*, etymologically linked to "obstetrics"). In Nigeria, at the edge of every Ibo village is a banana grove. Each tree is named after the child for whom it was planted and the plantation serves as the village playground.

If you decide to plant a birth tree for your baby, you could plant an ash for long life, a fig for wisdom or an olive for peace. A maple tree is traditionally said to bring good luck.

The Path of Destiny

A new baby is a mystery: who will she become? In the face of life's uncertainties people have devised many systems of predicting and explaining a child's destiny.

The time of birth has always played a pivotal role in systems of fate and prediction. In the Scottish Highlands certain days of the week are considered to be more auspicious than others: Tuesday's child will be "solemn and sad", while Wednesday's is "merry and glad". (Watch out for Thursday's child who is supposed to be "inclined to thieving"!) In Christian tradition a child is believed to be especially blessed if born on a Sunday. German mothers said that the Sabbath child grows up strong and

beautiful, while Scandinavians believed that Sunday's children could see spirits.

Filipino babies born at night are said to be braver than those born during the day. In Welsh folklore the infant born at sunrise is destined to be intelligent and successful, while the baby who emerges at sunset is inclined to be lazy and lacking in ambition. Traditional English custom, meanwhile, holds that children born at the hours of three, six, nine and twelve – when church bells traditionally chimed – will have the gift of prophecy, or "second sight". To be born during the incoming tide, a harbinger of new life, is often thought lucky in coastal regions.

In places where the weather changes swiftly, the conditions at the time of birth are said to affect the personality of the baby. In parts of the Philippines, it is said that children born on a sunny day will always be full of joy.

Ga women in western Africa say that the pregnant woman's environment shapes the temperament of her child. If she lives on plains of burnt grass, her child will be smooth-skinned and very dark. If she lives on a hill with distant views, her child will be tall and strong. Should she live near the sea, her

children will be as lively and loud as the crashing surf.

Many cultures have looked to the stars to reveal individual destiny. The position of the sun in the stars at the time of birth gives the child's zodiac sign and each sign is believed to carry certain personality traits (see page 62). Western astrologers also predict the patterns of a child's life by drawing up a "horoscope" – a chart showing the relative positions of the sun, moon, stars and planets with respect to the exact time and place of a person's birth. The horoscope will identify the heavenly influences at work throughout the child's life. Its interpretation will show the course that his life might take, including the kind of work to which he might be best suited; or the zodiac sign of his ideal partner.

The Chinese zodiac (see page 63) is based on a cyclical twelve-year system, which aligns each personality with a particular animal. In Chinese legend the twelve animals argued about who should be first in the cycle. The gods held a contest – whoever could reach the opposite riverbank first would have that privilege. As the animals leapt into the river, the Rat climbed onto the Ox's back. The Ox looked set to win, but just as he reached the bank, the Rat jumped ashore before him and so won the race.

THE WESTERN ZODIAC

Aries, The Ram
March 21 – April 19
Full of energy and enthusiasm, these children make great leaders.

Taurus, The Bull
April 20 – May 20
Cautious but practical children who are loyal to their friends.

Gemini, The Twins
May 21 – June 21
Bright, witty personalities who are apt to be fidgety, or chatterboxes.

Cancer, The Crab
June 22 – July 22
Sensitive and emotional children who like to care for others.

Leo, The Lion
July 23 – August 22
Like to be the centre of attention, but they are also loving and generous.

Virgo, The Maiden
August 23 – September 22
Often perfectionists, these children have keen analytical minds.

Libra, The Scales
September 23 – October 23
Harmonious children who love their friends, but can be a little lazy.

Scorpio, The Scorpion
October 24 – November 21
Powerful personalities who enjoy puzzles and mysteries – they are rarely ill.

Sagittarius, The Archer
November 22 – December 21
Sagittarius children have great insight and demand to be treated fairly.

Capricorn, The Goat
December 22 – January 19
Practical, serious children with ambition and drive.

Aquarius, The Water Carrier
January 20 – February 18
These children love anything new or different – they are easily bored.

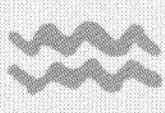

Pisces, The Fish
February 19 – March 20
Extremely inventive, sensitive children who need quiet times to themselves.

THE CHINESE ZODIAC

Years of the Rat (1984, 1996, 2008)
Rats are charming and ambitious.

Years of the Ox (1985, 1997, 2009)
Oxen are patient and confident.

Years of the Tiger (1986, 1998, 2010)
Tigers are sensitive and courageous.

Years of the Rabbit (1987, 1999, 2011)
Rabbits are articulate and clever.

Years of the Dragon (1988, 2000, 2012)
Dragons are energetic and soft-hearted.

Years of the Snake (1989, 2001, 2013)
Snakes are wise and intense.

Years of the Horse (1990, 2002, 2014)
Horses are popular and perceptive.

Years of the Sheep (1991, 2003, 2015)
Sheep are elegant and gentle.

Years of the Monkey (1992, 2004, 2016)
Monkeys are inventive and flexible.

Years of the Rooster (1993, 2005, 2017)
Roosters are capable and solitary.

Years of the Dog (1994, 2006, 2018)
Dogs are loyal and honest.

Years of the Pig (1995, 2007, 2019)
Pigs are studious and kind.

BIRTHSTONES

January – Garnet

February – Amethyst

March – Aquamarine

April – Diamond

May – Emerald

June – Pearl/Moonstone

July – Ruby

August – Peridot

September – Sapphire

October – Opal/Rose Zircon

November – Golden Topaz/Citrine

December – Turquoise/Blue Topaz

CHAPTER 3

Early Days

A baby is a question mark and his mother the answer he seeks. Sensitive to every new encounter, the newborn experiences life through the soft filter of his mother's embrace, her milk, her lullabies. He recognizes you by sight and by touch – you sense his needs and his separate self. Together, you will learn.

An Instinctive Connection

Some people say that there's no such thing as maternal instinct – for them the mysterious act of mothering is simply a bundle of skills that can be learned on the job – by anyone.

Of course, if we spend enough time with a baby, we may anticipate her needs – given the right care and attention from various sources, a baby will thrive. Yet biological and anthropological evidence (and common sense) support the idea that mothers are specifically suited to care for their own offspring. Women's bodies have evolved to accommodate the nine-month incubation of babies and their milk is adapted for long-term breast-feeding. These functions suggest that nature intended for mothers and babies to spend their time together, and in most societies, they do.

Mothering skills are not indelible, however: they can be honed or lost. For example, few Western women know when their babies

A MOTHER-AND-BABY HONEYMOON

We usually think of a honeymoon as a time of privacy for a husband and wife but, in many cultures, the tradition of undisturbed intimacy applies also to a mother and her baby immediately after the birth. The Wayãpo tribe of Brazil observe a "moon-long" seclusion for a newly delivered mother and child, during which time they bond with one another and learn each other's shapes and smells.

In India, according to ancient Ayurvedic principles, new mothers stay in their homes for the first twenty-two days after the birth. During this period, the mother-infant bond develops as the mother remains focused only on nurturing and getting to know her baby. Breastfeeding develops smoothly and naturally, free from pressure to clock-watch.

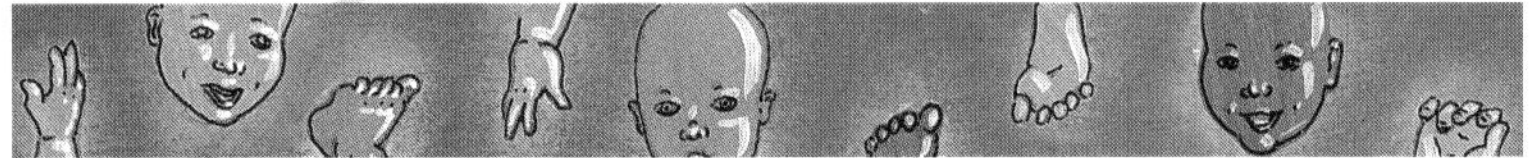

want to urinate, yet many babies around the world do not wear diapers or nappies. Instead, mothers hold the baby at arm's length. When a Netsilik woman was asked how she knew when to do this, she replied: "How could any mother be so dumb not to know?"

Many aspects of motherhood do not need to be taught. Studies show that pregnant women predict the weight of their babies more accurately than doctors or machines. First-time mothers put infants to the breast without the need for demonstration and rock their babies at sixty to seventy beats a minute, similar to the rhythm of the adult's heart; they also tend to carry infants on their left-hand side – near the maternal heartbeat. New mothers often recognize the sound of their own infant in a ward of crying babies, and most mothers can recognize the unique scent of their babies.

"There is no such thing as a baby, there is a baby and someone."

D.W. WINNICOTT (20TH-CENTURY BRITISH PSYCHOANALYST)

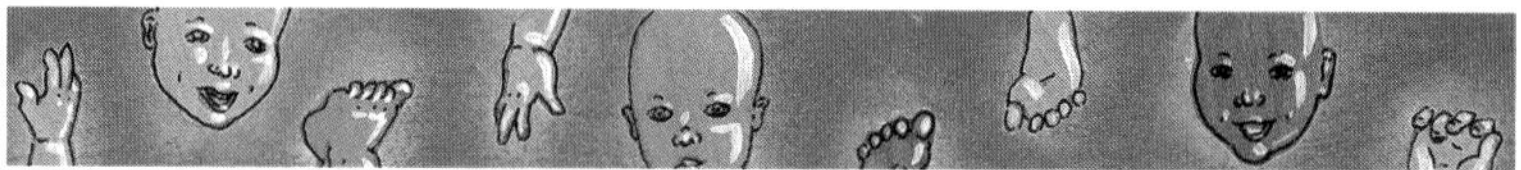

Besides the instinctive physical triggers, there are more mysterious aspects. Some mothers have a "sixth sense" when their children are in danger. They seem to have telepathic conversations and early-warning signs if their baby is becoming unwell – these are scientifically inexplicable. An intact maternal instinct surrounds a child like an aura, protecting her in countless subtle ways.

Many mothers expect to feel an immediate bond with their new baby and become anxious if instead they feel rather detached. For some, the connection begins before birth – a dream or an event may suddenly intensify feelings for the baby. But others do not feel instant adoration, even when the baby is finally in their arms. Of course, there are those who fall in love at first sight, but bonding is an intangible, highly personal process, and slow bonding is normal too.

Everyday acts of caring such as soothing your little one to sleep, or holding her to your breast, create the ties that will bind you for ever.

Everything Came from Her

"My early years are connected … with my mother. … I can remember the comforting feel of her body as she carried me on her back. … When I was hungry or thirsty she would swing me round to where I could reach her full breasts. … At night when there was no sun to warm me, her arms, her body took its place; and as I grew older … from my safe place on her back I could watch without fear as I wanted, and when sleep overcame me I had only to close my eyes."

KABONGO, AN EAST-AFRICAN KIKIYU CHIEF,
REMEMBERS HIS EARLY YEARS

Mothering the Mother

The first weeks after birth are an important time for a mother and baby. As well as being the honeymoon period (see box, page 67), this is a particularly crucial time for the mother in which to rest and recuperate. A new mother needs to be reassured and nurtured almost as much as her newborn baby.

In many cultures a new mother is exempt from her normal duties and is looked after by a team of family and friends. Special meals prepared for postnatal women are chosen for their special strength-giving properties. Sudanese women are brought daily gifts of goat's or camel's milk; in India, family members prepare nourishing lentil soups, and a concoction of nuts, raisins, lotus seeds and ghee is stored ready for the seclusion period. In Switzerland, newly delivered mothers were brought the first pickings from cherry trees – apart from being a delicious treat, this practice was thought to ensure a good cherry crop.

A traditional midwife often stays during the "honeymoon", to teach the mother about babycare and provide her with healing baths and

soothing massages. Ilocanos mothers in the Philippines are given a ritual bath in *a-nger* (boiled guava leaves) and regular abdominal massages. You may like to try a sitz bath with a few drops each of cypress and lavender essential oils, both of which aid healing and guard against infection. Moroccan mothers are massaged with henna, walnut bark and kohl; traditional Hawaiian midwives give a vigorous circular *lomi-lomi* massage with their fingers, elbows and thumbs.

Japanese women wear a *hari-obi* ("wide sash") in pregnancy to support the abdomen; they also wear it for about three weeks after birth to help them to get back into shape. To make your own, use a piece of cloth 8in (20cm) by 6ft, 6in (2m), wrapped three or four times around your lower back and stomach. Don't bind it too tightly – the idea is to support the uterus, not restrict circulation.

In some cultures this time of rest and recuperation is strictly imposed and surrounded by taboos. In Jewish law a mother is considered *nidoh* ("impure") for seven days after the birth of a boy and four days after a girl. After seven subsequent "clean" days she is ritually immersed in purifying water. Meanwhile, in European Christian tradition, women were "churched" a few weeks after childbirth. This process (a medieval ritual once practised all over the Christian world) was, in effect, a church service to welcome a new mother back into the heart of the community after her period of seclusion. She would return to society refreshed and relaxed, ready to show off her beautiful new baby – already secure in and trustful of his mother's arms.

Nature's Vaccine

Most people recognize the benefits of mother's milk, but what about the honey that comes first? The value of colostrum, "nature's vaccine", has been neglected for centuries.

This rich pre-milk is produced in late pregnancy and for three days after birth. It is nearly invisible – many mothers simply have to trust that they are producing it.

The sooner a baby begins suckling, the better: for a few hours after birth, colostrum contains enormous quantities of antibodies. On the first day it teems with fatty acids, growth factors, vitamins, zinc, immune defences and anti-infectious properties, and is particularly rich in vitamin A to supplement the low liver reserves of newborns. However, this potency is short-lived: as breast-milk replaces colostrum, protective cells decrease from millions to thousands. The Gusii tribe of Kenya value the colostrum, which, they say, "makes the child fat".

But in many places the demands of religion and medical theory cause the remarkable benefits of colostrum to be lost. In Bangladesh colostrum is known as "bad milk". Newborn babies are given honey and cow's milk until the mother begins to produce milk. Breton mothers in France traditionally do not feed their babies before baptism, which usually takes place when the baby is three days old.

Apart from the physical benefits to the new baby, the mother also profits psychologically by breastfeeding her baby from the outset. Successful breast-feeding often begins in the "practice" days before milk begins to flow.

Some mothers are encouraged to bottlefeed a new baby in order to maintain high blood-sugar levels. However, it is perfectly normal for a newborn to have low blood sugar for some hours after the birth – frequent breastfeeding soon improves the balance. Keep your baby near you with plenty of skin-to-skin contact. This will stimulate the "colostrum ejection reflex". Try to limit visitors until you are used to feeding your baby.

A Mother's Milk

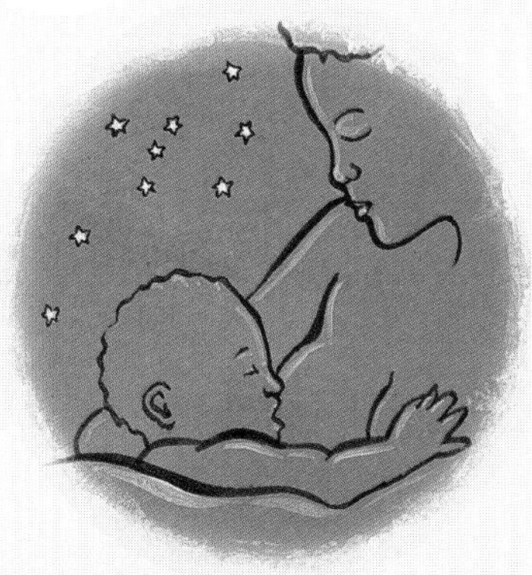

Breastfeeding is not just a form of nourishment – it is also a powerful and subtle form of communication, enhanced by stroking, playfulness and eye-contact. For your baby, it is a wonderful feast, engaging all her senses. A mother's natural food supply is also nutritionally ideal for the newborn.

Even in societies where babies are denied the breast for the first three days (for various reasons), mothers may go on to nurse until the child is two or three years old – or even older. While solids are also gradually introduced, breastfeeding provides an emotional continuum, a reassuring point of contact for both a mother and her baby.

Women among the !Kung hunter-gatherers of Botswana and Namibia follow a common breastfeeding pattern that was probably known to the earliest humans – and it works to the mutual benefit of baby and mother. Babies suckle briefly and often throughout the day and night, creating a perfect rhythm of supply and demand. Breastfeeding problems are extremely rare. Contraception is unknown, but the baby's suckling stimulates production of the breastfeeding hormone prolactin, which also suppresses ovulation. Hence, the frequent nursing helps to ensure a gap of up to four years between each child.

Although we may not be able to offer our babies the same level of skin-to-skin contact, we can learn from societies where breastfeeding is assumed to be normal. Difficult or uncomfortable breastfeeding is often the result of insufficient feeds or poor positioning of the baby (with gums on the nipple, rather than over the areola). Problems with breastfeeding occur mainly in cultures where mothers rarely see each other nursing. Girls who witness breastfeeding on a daily basis absorb the techniques unconsciously from an early age.

One of the keys to breastfeeding is the simple knowledge that every woman can do it. You do not need any equipment nor any special attributes. One useful piece of information to aid trouble-free breastfeeding is that the nipples are best left unwashed – soap spoils the

natural aroma of your skin to which your baby is attuned. Washing with soap also reduces the moisture of the areola.

If problems do occur, there are countless traditional remedies. Mothers in southeast Asia believe that they can increase their milk supply by eating the flowers of a banana tree and nourishing chicken broth. To prevent their nipples from becoming dry, Taralpe women of Brazil moisturize them with honey; alternatively, the

Magar of Nepal use apricot oil. If your breasts become engorged (too full), try the old European remedy of cabbage leaves, with holes cut for the nipples. Apply cold, raw leaves after each feed (they will fit snugly inside a bra), and leave them against your breasts until the leaves have reached room temperature. Cracked nipples also respond to a treatment that couldn't be easier to find – moisturize them with a few drops of breastmilk.

THE BIRTH OF THE MILKY WAY

According to Greek legend, the hero Heracles was born to the mortal Alcmene, as a result of her secret liaison with the god Zeus. After his labours on earth, Heracles ascended to Olympus to become an Immortal. He was "reborn" to Hera, goddess of marriage and maternity, in an adoption ritual once practised by barbarian tribes. Hera went to bed in mock labour and "produced" baby Heracles from under the sheets. However, having been born originally to a mortal mother, Heracles had yet to achieve true immortality. Zeus placed him secretly in Hera's bed to suckle her divine milk. Unaware of his strength, Heracles sucked so eagerly that Hera's milk spilled across the night sky, creating the phenomenon we know as the Milky Way.

Protecting the Newborn

Newborn babies are universally believed to be vulnerable creatures – in many cultures the dangers are seen to be spiritual as well as physical. Protective charms are often considered as important as medicine and common sense to ensure the safety of a newborn baby.

In European tradition, boys are dressed in blue, girls in pink. Blue, the sacred colour of the heavens, was traditionally used as a divine and magical shield for male infants. (Girls, who were less desirable to the evil spirits, wore pink, the colour of European skin.) Evidence of the belief in the magical power of blue is also found in the Middle East, where an entire household – including the new baby in it – was safeguarded by painting the front door a brilliant blue.

"... to make you strong and fair and always young and to keep back death and sorrow, and to keep you safe from other winds and evil spirits."

AN IRISH WOMAN'S PRAYER AS SHE HOLDS UP A NEW BABY TO THE SOUTH WIND

Among the Native American Hopi tribe, sacred corn ears are placed on either side of the baby's cradle for the first twenty days of her life. In ancient Rome a nine-day-old baby was given a *bulla* – a rounded metal or leather box containing a charm to ward off evil spirits. The child would keep the *bulla* until she made the transition to adulthood at puberty. In ancient Egypt the cat goddess Bastet was the guardian of all infants, and during childbirth her image was worn on necklaces to safeguard both mother and child.

An *Ojo de Dios*, "God's Eye", was an ancient talisman made by the Huichol people of Mexico. You might like to try making one of your own. You need two straight twigs and various coloured yarns. Form a cross-shape with the sticks and, using some yarn, bind them with diagonal strokes in both directions across the centre. This is the "iris" of the *Ojo de Dios*, ready to protect your new baby. At each birthday, tie on a new colour, wrapping it over and under each spoke around the cross, until the fifth birthday when the charm is complete, giving you a memento to treasure.

Sleep, Baby, Sleep

In Central America, each newborn baby has a *nahual*, or animal twin, which protects him during sleep. To discover the beast's identity, a circle of ashes is placed around the baby's sleeping place, in which the *nahual* leaves tell-tale footprints. A taboo is proclaimed against killing the beast and, in return, the *nahual* becomes the child's lifelong protector.

By night as by day, traditional societies ensure magical protection for their babies. Nightmares are particularly frightening for children and have been widely believed to be caused by malevolent spirits. In ancient Greece parents would spend a night with their baby in the temple of Hypnos (the god of sleep) to be sure of the god's protection against night-time visitations by evil spirits. In Eastern

FENG SHUI FOR THE SLEEPING PLACE

The Chinese believe that energy (*qi*) flows through everything around us. When this energy is blocked, we feel unease. Feng Shui is the ancient technique for organizing our surroundings to maximize energy flow and so create well-being. The practice can easily be applied to a baby's sleeping place to enhance peaceful sleep.

The door of a baby's bedroom should always be left open to allow energy to flow easily into and out of the room. However, the cradle, cot or family bed should never be placed in the direct line of incoming energy (directly opposite the door), as this is said to disturb the baby's sleep. Try positioning your baby's sleeping place against a wall with the doorway in sight, so that he can see whoever is coming into the room. Avoid placing a baby's bed beneath a window, as the passage from door to window is an energy highway, which could cause interruption to your baby's restful sleep.

According to the principles of Feng Shui, the walls of a baby's bedroom should be decorated predominantly in the colour associated with the baby's Chinese birth element. If your baby is born into the wood element, the room should be blue; into fire, green; into earth, red; into metal, yellow; and into water, white. You could decorate the room with pictures of your baby's Chinese birth animal (see page 63).

If there is a mirror in the room, don't place it opposite the foot of the cradle or bed, or directly opposite the door. Positive energy travelling through the room will be reflected onto the resting baby, and this may disrupt his sleep.

Europe mothers would place a small broom under the baby's pillow, to sweep away evil spirits; and Romanies tucked sprigs of rosemary under the pillow to ensure sweet dreams. English cradles were often made of ash wood, which was said to have protective qualities.

As they grow children of many cultures share their beds with their siblings or other family members for safety and warmth. In the Dani tribe of Irian Jaya, men and boys sleep together on large mats and wake often during the night. They tell a story or stoke the fire, then doze off again.

Many traditions imply that the baby has his own sleeping place – a crib in the parent's room or, as in most modern Western homes, in a different room altogether. However, there are a significant number of cultures in which a newborn baby is brought into the parental bed to sleep beside his mother, where her familiar presence, the warmth of her body, her smell and her caresses all help the baby to sleep easily, as he did in the womb. Infant sleep disturbance and adult insomnia are rare in places where parents and babies "co-sleep".

DREAMCATCHING

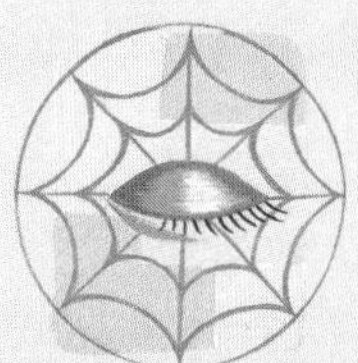

Dreamcatchers are hanging dream filters, traditionally made by Lakota Native Americans and suspended near the sleeping place. The dreamcatcher traps nightmares within its web and allows sweet dreams to pass through.

To make a traditional dreamcatcher (as wide as an average adult hand), you will need approximately 4ft (1.2m) of soaked willow bough (or grapevine) and 10ft (3m) of strong, thin string. Bend the willow to create a hoop of double thickness, and bind it where the ends meet.

Tie the string onto the hoop, leaving a short loose end to make a loop for hanging (call this point on the hoop twelve o'clock). Take the long end of the string and stretch the string along the hoop to two o'clock. Make a knot by winding the string over the hoop to the back, then bringing it to the front through the hole between string and hoop. Pull it taut, and continue around the hoop, making knots at four, six, eight and ten o'clock. For the subsequent rounds, make the knots around the previous round of string instead of the hoop. As you pull gently, the spaces between your knots will form a web.

On the third round, add a bead to represent the spider in the web. When the stitches become too small to pass the string through, leave a hole in the centre and finish with a knot, allowing 6–8in (15–20cm) of string to tie on two or three feathers. The dreamcatcher should reflect the person it protects – attach thread from your baby's scarf or a favourite teddy's ribbon. Beads and feathers added at a new moon increase the magic.

Rock-A-Bye Baby

Sung by mothers and nurses all over the world to coax babies to sleep, lullabies use the soft hum and gentle rhythm of simple tunes and phrases to re-create for the baby a sense that she is safe in the womb. Combined with gentle rocking, lullabies give the reassuring message: drift off to sleep, mother is here, all is well with the world.

ENGLAND

Sweet and low, sweet and low,
Wind of the western sea.
Low, low, breathe and blow –
Wind of the western sea!
Over the rolling waters go;
Come from the dying moon and blow,
Blow him again to me;
While my little one, while my pretty
one, sleeps.

RUSSIA

Sleep, ah sleep, my darling baby,
Su, su, lullaby.
See the moon is watching o'er thee,
Peacefully on high.
Thou shalt hear a wondrous story,
Close each wakeful eye,
And a song as well I'll sing thee,
Su, su, lullaby.

CREOLE

Go to sleep, Colas little Brother,
Go to sleep, sweet dreams be with you.
Mamma will bake a sweet little cake,
Papa's here with choc'late for you.
Go to sleep, Colas little brother
Go to sleep, sweet dreams be with you.

USA

Hushabye, don't you cry,
Go to sleep, little baby.
Mammy's here, have no fear,
Here to watch her little baby.
Sleep and rest,
Mammy's blest
Mammy's blest little baby.

GERMANY

Sleep, baby, sleep,
Your father tends the sheep,
Your mother shakes the little bough,
A dream falls gently on you now,
Sleep, baby, sleep.

The Power of Touch

Born into a confusing world, with simple, primitive needs, all babies respond to human touch – scientists call this "skin hunger". Babies are designed to be physically appealing: a baby's soft skin makes us want to stroke, kiss and protect him. When a baby gives vent to an anguished wail he is often literally crying out to be held.

The Mundugumor of New Guinea raise their children with the minimum of contact. Infants are carried in baskets suspended from the mother's forehead, and at weaning they are pushed away from the breast and smacked. These actions may contribute to the aggressive behaviour valued by the tribe. But most cultures aim to encourage loving touch in their children. Babies' lives are shaped by the hands that hold them, and it is within our power to raise children who love to be held and to hold. The Filipino Tasay tribe live in a loving community, and the importance of touch is passed on through the generations. Babies are constantly stroked and held – even the adults sit arm in arm and nuzzle one another. The principles are so simple yet so effective: massage your baby, stroke his face as he feeds, and hold him in your arms as often as you can.

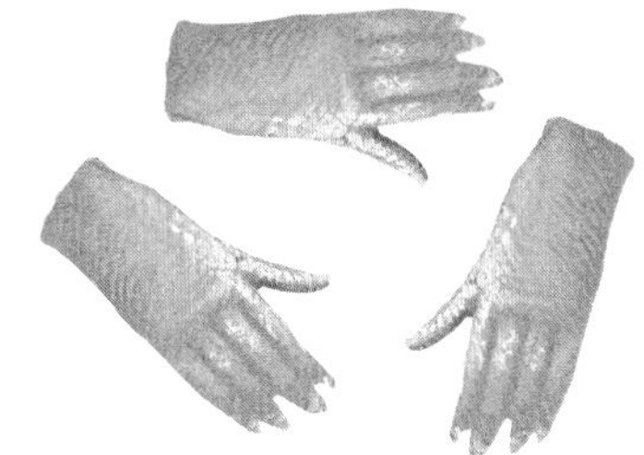

BABY MASSAGE

Life in the womb is like a nine-month flotation, combined with an all-over body massage. Soothing massages can make a fractious newborn feel safe again. In India, where all children are massaged regularly, the art is passed down from mother to daughter; in Russian hospitals mothers are taught massage to stimulate the baby's immature nervous system. Moroccan babies are massaged with henna and butter, or an aromatic mixture including marjoram and mint. Nyinba babies in Nepal are massaged twice daily with mustard-seed oil and breastmilk.

Try giving your baby a gentle massage – a good time is after a warm bath and before sleep. First, spend time simply holding. When you are ready to begin, make sure that your hands are not cold. Find a position that suits you both: your baby might lie against your chest, or with his back propped up on your raised thighs.

Smooth your baby's body with a light film of almond massage oil. (Essential oils are best avoided for baby massage.) Intuition is your best guide. Use your fingertips and keep all movements feather-light. Softly slide your hands in opposite directions across his stomach, and rotate your fingers clockwise around his belly button. Massage his legs, arms, fingers and toes. Avoid the cord stump, and do not pull on his limbs. Above all, watch and listen to your baby. If he becomes restless, he's had enough. Ten minutes of magical contact with his mother may be all he needs.

Tears and Smiles

The crying comes first – a yell of anguish is usually the first signal of life. A baby's first breath takes five times more energy than all the other breaths to come. According to Native American Osage mothers, this cry is a prayer that the baby learned before her spirit descended to earth – she is calling to Grandfather Sun and Moon Woman to ask for their protection in her new world.

In many cultures a baby is encouraged to cry lustily to prove herself healthy. In Haiti it was the custom for a large wooden bowl to be held upside-down over a sleepy newborn. This was beaten like a drum to make the baby wake up with a wail of distress. Until recently Western doctors would hold babies up by their ankles and smack them to produce a loud cry and unblock the airways.

Other societies place emphasis on a gentle birth. French birth pioneer Frédéric Leboyer took many of his ideas from ancient India. Subtle lighting, whispering voices and the reassurance of the mother's body make it possible for some babies to be born without crying. The first breath is a sudden reflex, air rushes in and the baby exclaims. She is surprised, but not necessarily distressed.

A new baby does not weep real tears until around three weeks old, but her crying is a whole body experience – a rhythmical wail and a face completely distorted in the spasm of her own torment. All over the world, mothers soothe their crying babies by holding, suckling, rocking and singing to them. In Jamaica, as in many other cultures, older siblings are given the task of soothing the baby; girls stop their infant brother or sister from crying by strapping them to their backs and carrying them along as they play.

Among the Ibo peoples of western Africa, a newborn's cries are said to be plaintive songs to the unborn children whom he has left far behind in the spirit world.

In New Mexico women of the Seri tribe have a solution for persistently crying babies. They take some twigs from the nest of a bird known as "the bird who sleeps in the afternoon". These are burned on four small fires placed at four corners around the restless child. As the smoke rises from the flame, her mother sings an incantation, calling on the bird's spirit to ease her crying.

However much a baby cries, her smiles are rarely very far behind. At first, these magical, happy faces are merely reflexes – fleeting expressions, which may start to appear when your baby is as young as three days old. According to an old Welsh tradition, when a baby smiles or laughs in her sleep, the fairies are kissing her. Soon, however, your baby offers her first real smile, a four-week-old expression of delight. The smiles become longer and broader, until, at somewhere between four and seven months, she gives her first specific,

intentional and affectionate smile. Now she is ready to laugh.

Laughter is perilously close to crying, a signal of relief, often resulting from potentially scary games like "peek-a-boo" or tickling. A laughing baby sends the powerful message: "I know I am safe with you." When she realizes that she is in safe hands, her cry becomes a chuckle. Soon, she wants to repeat this pleasurable experience, turning anticipated fear into sheer joy.

Children of the Sky

When babies are born in twos, they bring twice the magic. Along the parched coastline of Delagoa Bay, in southeast Africa, twins of the Baronga tribe and their mothers are attributed with the power to bring rain. A mother of twins is known as Tilo, "The Sky", and her twins are known as "Children of the Sky". In spring, if the rains are late, Baronga women conduct a ritual to encourage the precious rain to fall. They put on grass skirts and sing wild songs; then they call at a house where twins have been born. Although fresh water is scarce, they drench the mother of twins with water carried in pitchers. Now that the Sky – a mother imbued with twin magic – is wet, the rains will come.

More twins are born to African mothers than to any other race in the world – one in every twenty-two African pregnancies is expected to result in twins. For the North Americans and Europeans, this figure is one in a hundred, and one in two hundred for the Japanese.

Twin births are surrounded with mystery and superstition. Some tribes assume that a woman must have had sex with two men at around the same time. Others see

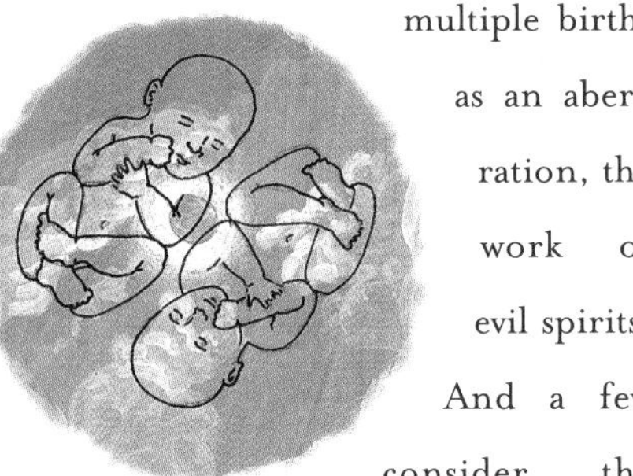

multiple births as an aberration, the work of evil spirits. And a few consider the intimacy of twins in the womb an impropriety which must be rectified – in Japan and the Philippines, boy-girl twins were traditionally required to marry each other when they came of age.

Although twins were considered undesirable by some (the Navaho Native Americans likened twins to the litters of lower animals), elsewhere they were regarded as a great blessing. Kings of Benin would donate to any mother of twins the services of a royal wet nurse to indicate his pleasure at their arrival. Ewe women of West Africa wear a special badge to announce proudly that they have had twins. You could join them by making your own "Mother of Twins" badge (if you get a spare minute).

In places where twins are believed to have magical powers, they are often accorded special treatment. Among the Ga people of Africa, great efforts are made to meet their every request to avoid causing them anger. Every year a *yeleyeli*, or thanksgiving yam-feast, is held in honour of the pampered pair. The next child to be born is named Tawia – the Ga believe that he or she has been "sent" by the

gods in order to serve the twins; and Tawia must spend his or her life in devotion to their many and varied needs. Unsurprisingly, Ga parents regard twins as something of a mixed blessing.

On a practical level, twins need skilful management. Their births can be more complicated and their early lives can cause physical, practical and economic strain on daily family life. But as most "sky" mothers will testify, they also bring more than double the delight. Who knows? Perhaps they may even bring the spring rain.

THE ONLY CHILD

In many parts of the world, solitary children are rare. But in China, where government policy limits parents to one child, and in the West, where birth control is widely used, many families have only children. In America and Europe, for example, only children were five times more common in the 1990s than they were during the previous decade. Popular myth holds that a solitary child will be self-centred and inflexible, and is more likely to get divorced. But an intense upbringing with lots of praise (as well as lots of blame) need not cause problems – only children are usually conscientious and loyal. In European fairy tales only children leave home to seek their fortune, returning with untold wealth. The moral may be that parents should take care to give their only child freedom to flourish fully.

CHAPTER 4

Your Baby Grows

The intense togetherness of the early months must fade, but the passage through childhood brings with it new joys and challenges. As your baby grows her unique character will emerge, along with her own preferences and perspective on the world. As a parent you will soon learn to balance your protective instincts with giving your child enough freedom to become her own person.

First Foods

A baby's first taste of "real" food traditionally comes from his mother's milk, which absorbs and dilutes the flavours of the food that she eats. So breastfed babies start attuning to their future diet from the minute they take their first feed. Thai babies enjoy breastmilk infused with traces of lemon grass and galangal root, and older Indian babies may even be perfectly content to eat spicy curry. Recent research indicates that bottle-fed babies (who will not have had the benefit of food-traces in their mother's own milk) are less willing to accept solid food.

In some cultures babies are given their first solid food soon after birth. Among the Karen tribe of northern Thailand, babies are fed a few grains of rice and told: "This is what you will be eating in a year's time." Babies in northern

Canada and Greenland were traditionally given some meat at birth to initiate them into the cycle of exchange between humans and nature – it was believed that animals willingly gave up their lives in exchange for correct ritual observance. Whether or not the baby ate the food was unimportant. The infant was not considered to be fully human until he had joined the meat-sharing community.

Many babies have a combined diet of breastmilk and solid food until the age of two or three. According to numerous cultural and medicinal traditions, the shift to solid foods is best made slowly to avoid losing the physical and emotional

benefits of breastfeeding. In some tribal societies babies are breastfed for up to five or six years – the length of time breastmilk is designed to be fed to an infant. However, in some cultures weaning takes place after a few months. In Western society this might be because the mother needs to return to work.

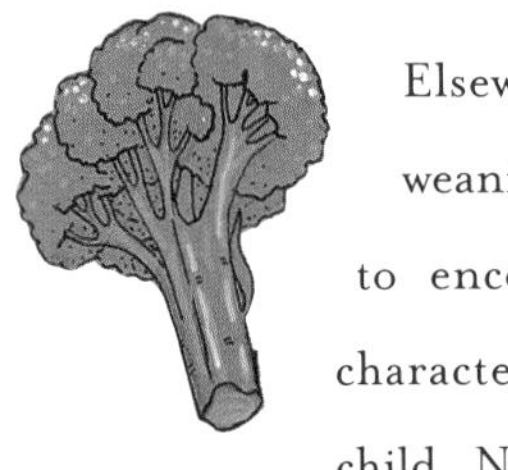

Elsewhere, sudden weaning is believed to encourage certain characteristics in the child. Native American Plains tribes used a method of abrupt breast denial in the belief that doing so encouraged an aggressive temperament in the children, which in later life made them fierce and formidable warriors.

In some cultures, methods of weaning can take the form of active deterrents. In Mexico, Aztec mothers called a sudden halt to breastfeeding by smearing their nipples with crushed chillies. The process of weaning is also very rapid in Java, Indonesia – mothers simply leave their child with a relative and return to collect him a few days later.

Tchumbuli infants in New Guinea are lured from the breast with sweet temptations, not sharp shocks. Mothers feed them sugar cane and lotus stems to encourage them to try solid food.

In the West, many of us take for granted the ease and accessibility of a liquidizer with which we can pulp numerous varieties of readily available foods. First foods vary greatly from one culture to

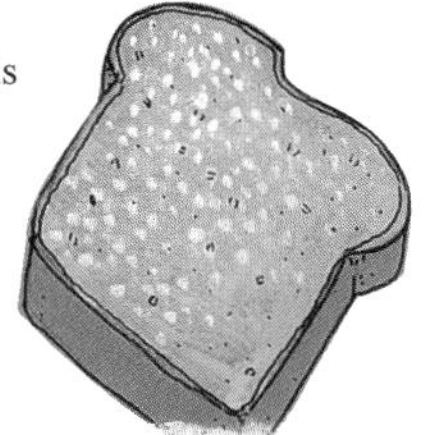

another, generally consisting of whatever items are fresh, local and easily digested: African babies might begin with mashed banana; while babies from the Mediterranean regions with mashed avocado. In many indigenous tribes, instead of mashing with kitchen equipment, mothers employ the traditional "kiss-feeding" method. The food is chewed into a pulp in the mother's own mouth before she gently transfers it to her baby's mouth with a kiss.

The Gift of Language

The Latin word *infans*, from which we derive the word "infant", means "he who is unable to speak". But all mothers know that communication begins long before actual speech. Babies "talk" to us with their eyes, their expressions and their whole bodies, and we respond to them in the same language.

A baby can hear conversations even while she is in the womb. As soon as she is born, she begins to filter the rhythms of speech and gradually recognizes meaning.

The best way to encourage your baby's language is to strike up a two-way conversation. Mothers all over the world talk to their babies in a special language known as "baby talk". Without learning how, we tend to use the simplest words and make sentences shorter. Mothers talk of themselves in the third person, speak more slowly, repeat things, and speak to their babies in a sing-song pitch (children learn more easily through rhythm and song). By looking at our babies while we talk to them, we also teach them the facial expressions that accompany speech.

MAMA PAPA

Babies start to babble from around three months, repeating easy syllables like "da", "ta", "ma", "ba" and "pa". All around the world, these first basic sounds form the roots of common names for other family members, most importantly "mother" and "father". For example, *baba* means "mother" among the Gusii tribe of Kenya, while *baban* is "father" for the Sambarivo people of Madagascar. The English word "daddy" is *tata* in Greek, and *papa* in French.

Considering the amount of time she spends with her newborn in the first months, a mother might expect her baby to say her name first. But this rarely happens. Studies have shown that, from Africa to Slovenia, babies try to name their fathers before their mothers. Perhaps father, a familiar but often slightly more distant figure, is considered more worthy of mention (mother is just the fixture who meets the baby's every need). Or perhaps mothers deliberately choose to interpret their baby's first word as "daddy", in order to make a father feel important.

In Europe the origins of the colloquial words for mother are intimately connected with breastfeeding. Mom, Mam, Mummy, Maman, Mutti, Mama – all these words derive from the ancient Greek *mamman*, which means "to cry for the breast", and the Roman *mamma*, meaning "breast".

Before you know it your baby will be giving her own special names to her brothers and sisters and the cat. But it's hardly surprising that a baby's very first syllables are directed at her parents – the first and foremost objects of a baby's attention.

Once Upon a Time

Many Western parents have lost faith in their ability to tell a story without a script. Yet children are appreciative listeners and enjoy the simplest of attempts. To rediscover the ancient skills of oral history, try retelling simple family events.

A child's inner world needs regular exercise. Television and picture books do too much of the work, stunting the powers of the imagination. Tell a child a story, and he will create his own screen of pictures, as vivid for him as everyday life. To an open-hearted child, fables and fairy stories transport him into realms of limitless possibility, where good and evil, or bravery and cowardice, do battle.

Stories teach, entertain and forge a unique bond between the teller and the child. In many societies young people learn their cultural heritage from stories. The Swedish poet Selma Lagerlf said that her grandmother would end fairy stories by saying: "All this is true, as I can see you and you are seeing me."

THE ART OF STORYTELLING

Between the ages of two and three, children love to hear stories about things that they know: retellings of their daily routines and familiar people help them to build up trust. You can tell your child stories about almost anything in his world: ducks in the park, the cat next door. Children also respond to the repetition and rhythm of nursery rhymes, and will love to hear your childhood stories.

Around the age of four, children are ready to enter fully into worlds of make-believe. You could begin by reading stories from books, but all children love to be told special stories invented just for them. Anthologies of traditional folk and fairy tales, such as those by the German Brothers Grimm, or from the *Arabian Nights*, offer a valuable source of inspiration.

Memorizing a tale, as all traditional storytellers do, is not as difficult as you might think. Read the story several times out loud and visualize the action. Practise retelling each part. Adapt the storyline of any fairy tale for your own child by introducing familiar figures or places from his life.

Try modifying your voice to bring your story alive: whisper secrets, and use croaky sounds for dangerous characters. Make eye contact with your child and use facial expressions for emphasis. You are literally an actor playing all the part and your child is the captivated audience.

Tooth Tales

Teeth are landmarks on the path from infancy to adulthood, but their schedules of arrival and departure vary from child to child. One in 2,000 babies is born with a tooth, yet there are one-year-olds who seem to manage with empty gums. Count your child's teeth on her first birthday – an old English tradition holds that the number reveals how many brothers and sisters she will have.

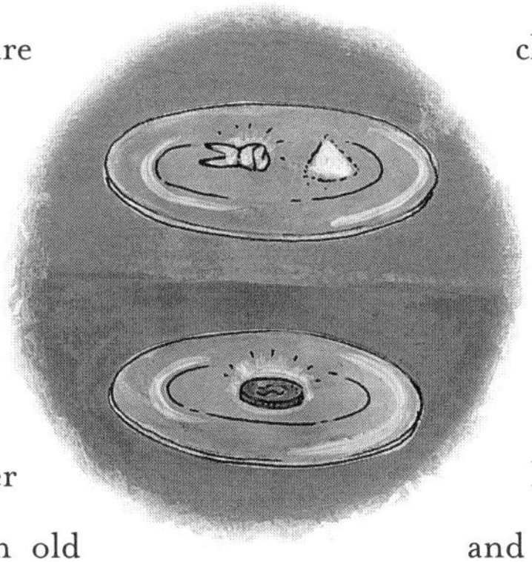

A child's first tooth is a milestone that mothers everywhere anticipate with great eagerness. In Uganda the Dhagga tribe holds a special ritual for its arrival. "Now," they say, "the child is complete." Grandma rubs herbs into the baby's gums, blesses her to encourage a healthy set of teeth and gives her a first taste of solid food.

First teeth (usually the four front teeth) cause few problems for

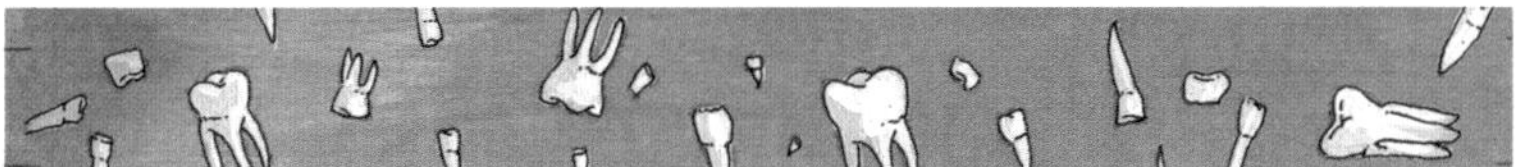

babies, but the arrival of molars may make them miserable. To ease teething pains, rub maple syrup mixed with a few drops of chamomile oil into your baby's gums. You could also try massaging the web of skin between the thumb and index finger (the acupressure point for toothache). It is a myth that teething causes fever and rashes, but keep a look out for one bright red cheek and excessive dribbling.

Children's teeth usually appear two by two, upper incisors followed by the lower pair. At the age of six or seven, children lose their "milk" (or "baby") teeth to make room for their adult set. Chinese children bury their upper baby teeth in the ground, to encourage their upper adult teeth to grow downward, while they throw their lower baby teeth over the roof of the house, so that their bottom adult teeth will shoot upward.

Many children are recompensed for the loss of baby teeth. In Britain each fallen tooth is placed under the child's pillow or on a plate with some salt. As the child sleeps, the "tooth fairy" exchanges the tooth for a coin. It is sometimes said

that the transfer must take place before midnight or bad luck will follow. In Italian tradition children leave their baby teeth in the fireplace. During the night a "mouse" takes the tooth away and leaves a sweet, or a coin, in its place. In homes without a fireplace, teeth are left on the window sill, and these days a coin, rather than a sweet, is the more common reward. In Spain gifts are left under the child's pillow by Ratoncito Perez, "Perez, the little mouse", in exchange for baby teeth. Balinese parents hold joyful

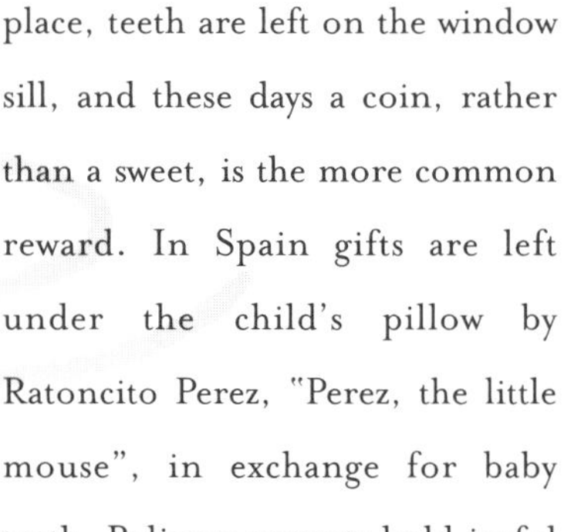

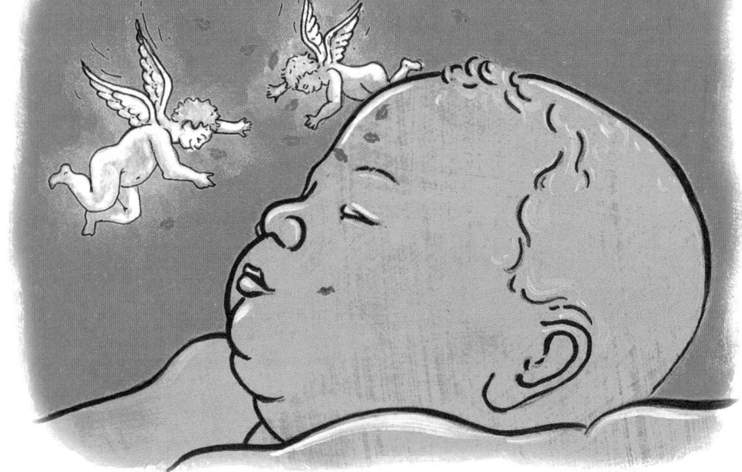

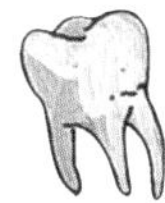

ceremonies to mark the loss of baby teeth. When adult teeth arrive the child is said to have completed the long transition from the spirit to the human world. Some people say that the change of teeth is a mini-adolescence for a child. Watch out for mood swings and sensitivity.

The setting of teeth in a child's mouth also has its own lore. In Scottish tradition a gap between the two front teeth is considered lucky; but if all the teeth are set too widely apart, it means that in the future the child will have to leave her home town to seek her fortune.

PROTECTING THE IVORY TOWERS

Brushing teeth morning and night with toothpaste is a ritual most common in Western societies, which have a love affair with refined sugar. Norwegian children are taught to fear TanVerk Trollet, the toothache troll, who will move into their mouths if they neglect to brush their teeth. But in Zaire sweets, and so tooth decay, are extremely rare. Children clean their teeth with chew sticks, which they break off from the Peelu or "toothbrush" tree.

Until your child is six or seven, she will probably need help with cleaning her teeth. You could encourage regular brushing by joining in at the same time. Most children love to take part in activities with their parents (at this early age) – and your own teeth will benefit, too!

Marking Time

In the West traditional birthday celebrations have been handed down from the birthday rituals of the ancient Greeks. Our elaborate birthday cake, in its original form, was simply round and white to honour the full moon – a symbol of regeneration and growth.

Evil spirits were traditionally thought to linger at birthday celebrations, and rituals to ward them off still survive. In England the birthday child is given "the bumps" (her friends grasp the child's arms and legs and lift her high into the air for each year of her life, ending with a gentle bump on the ground); in Scotland she is given a soft birthday punch; and in Belgium, to wake her up, she is given a gentle needle prick.

Not all cultures regard calendar time as the most significant marker of a child's growth. In Samoa celebratory feasts are held when babies learn how to sit, crawl and stand. Elsewhere rituals such as head-shaving, ear-piercing and circumcision mark the transition from childhood to adulthood.

Nevertheless, celebrating the anniversary of a child's birth is the most widely practised method of marking growth. If you have a birthday party for your child, you could adapt the following game from Central America. In the original game, the birthday child has to break the *piñata*, a decorated bag of treats which is attached to a rope, suspended from a beam or hook in the ceiling. Ask your guests to stand in a line while you suspend the *piñata* appropriately and securely. Let each guest take a turn at trying to break the *piñata* – if you fill the bag with sweets, then everyone can share the *piñata*'s gifts.

THE CANDLE OF LIFE

When you light your child's birthday candles, you are actually celebrating her safe journey through another year. The ritual dates back to medieval Germany, when birthday candles were kept alight all day. Eventually German families introduced small candles to put on top of the birthday cake – one for each year, plus one for the day of birth. This extra birthday flame is the Candle of Life. If a child could blow all her candles out at once, symbolically wiping out the past and starting afresh, her wish would be granted (as long as it was kept secret). The candle smoke was believed to carry her secret desire to the heavens.

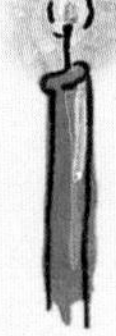

Some German children are given a twelve-year-candle as a christening present. You could decorate a large candle for your own child, using a pen and stickers to mark twelve stages. On each birthday let the candle burn down to the next line to show the relevant year.

CHAPTER 5

The Sisterhood of Mothers

Mothers are the guardians of life – they embody the mysterious regeneration that sustains all humanity. Their wealth of inherited wisdom is transmitted down through the generations, from mother to daughter, all over the world. Motherhood is a common cause, a universal and cherished gift, and an experience to share.

A Mother's Many Roles

Deep in the Amazon, where Kayapó Indians have lived relatively undisturbed for centuries, the roles of men and women are starkly divided. Men hunt and fish for food. And the women undertake almost everything else. They cultivate and harvest crops; gather, distribute and cook food; and hand-spin cotton. During all the household chores, they care for the children, carrying their smallest babies on their backs.

Wash on Monday
Iron on Tuesday
Mend on Wednesday
Churn on Thursday
Clean on Friday
Bake on Saturday
Rest on Sunday

A TRADITIONAL ENGLISH MOTHER'S WEEK

In male-dominated tribal societies (such as many Australian Aboriginal groups), as well as in societies where women enjoy sexual equality (among the !Kung tribe of Botswana, for example), women also often seem to do the bulk of the work. In most hunter-gatherer tribes, the women provide most of the food: they breastfeed the babies, gather edible roots and berries and catch

small animals to sustain their families on a daily basis. The masculine activity of game-hunting is a risky and time-consuming process, requiring the manufacture of weapons and long expeditions. But it is not relied upon as a family's primary source of nourishment.

In societies such as these, mothering has to be regarded more as a sideline rather than an all-consuming task – survival depends upon the flexibility of the community, including mothers. Breastfeeding continues throughout other daily activities and babies are carried around all day in slings, freeing up their mothers' arms and hands for other tasks.

Women in tribal cultures develop many special skills in addition to household and mothering work. Native American women are highly skilled in a wide variety of crafts such as weaving, sewing, beadwork, wood carving, midwifery and herbal medicine. Few tribal women give up these skills to devote themselves to motherhood – childcare is shared.

In Western society, too, the role of mother lies far beyond simply looking after the children. Even though the boundaries between a mother's and father's roles are now less defined, it still usually falls to the mother to undertake the essential household chores and be the primary caregiver. In addition many women find themselves (through necessity or for self-fulfilment) having to take a regular job. As a

result, many working mothers feel torn between their competing roles. Better nursery care and more flexible working environments are helping to bridge the gap between motherhood and career, but mothers everywhere are still having to juggle their other commitments and tasks with childcare.

A mother's many roles can be all-consuming, so it is important that you take time to relax and congratulate yourself on a regular basis: to be a mother is to be a superwoman, and you deserve to be pampered every now and then.

YOUR OWN TIME AND SPACE

Some new mothers find it hard to take time for themselves without feeling guilty, but it is important not to let the many roles of motherhood overwhelm you physically and emotionally. Just a few minutes of calm can restore your sense of inner peace.

While your child is sleeping, try a three-minute meditation. Count slowly from one to four, breathing in deeply as you do so. Exhale in one long, slow out-breath. Do this five times. Be careful not to over-breathe.

Immersing yourself in warm water is a wonderful way to escape. While your partner or a friend is on hand to childmind, take a luxurious bath. Sprinkle a few drops of lavender oil in the water. Rest your head on a towel, close your eyes, let your body dissolve into the water and unwind.

If You Teach a Woman

"If you teach a man you teach one person;

if you teach a woman you teach a whole family."

TRADITIONAL SAYING FROM KERALA, SOUTHERN INDIA

The Mother-Line

The art and skills of motherhood are transmitted subtly through the generations. As one British grandmother highlights, "I only realized the power of the mother-line when I heard my daughter singing a lullaby to her baby – it was a lullaby taught to me by my own grandmother."

Girls all over the world spend much of their early childhood watching their mothers, absorbing their example and imitating their tasks. When new babies are born, older girls often carry them and care for them, earning the title "little mother".

Among the Zaramo of Tanzania, continuity between the generations of women is nurtured and guarded with pride. Girls stay close to the women in the household throughout their childhood and participate in all their work. They follow their mothers to fetch water from the well, balancing small tins on their heads until they are old enough to manage large water pots. Later on they plant, tend and harvest crops, and look after their younger siblings. They learn to weave colourful hats and braid hair into intricate plaits; these crafts are shrouded in secrecy from men,

and this fosters an atmosphere of mystery and pride in the whole sphere of "women's work".

Zaramo families consider the birth of a girl to be lucky, as one day she will bring bride-wealth to the family and ensure the continuation of the mother's line (which takes precedence over the father's). As a gesture of respect to the mother's parents, a firstborn girl is named after her maternal grandmother, and the girl is believed to share some of her grandmother's personal qualities.

In the Lebanon when five generations of women from the same family gather together, it is called *Ya sette kellme settik* ("Oh grandmother speak to your grandmother"). The physical gathering of the mother-line – a daughter with her mother, grandmother, great-grandmother, and so on – represents a vast store of mothering wisdom and experience.

Of course, knowledge and experience are only passed on if the values of the past are respected. Honouring elders and ancestors is a vital aspect of tribal life, where survival depends upon continuity. In Maori culture children are often given to their grandparents to be raised in a traditional way.

But we live in a world that often disregards or rejects its recent history. Many Western women vow to do things differently from their own mothers, believing that they

can do better. We often raise our children to have aspirations outside the home, rather than within it. Although becoming a mother is increasingly a life choice in the West, rather than an inevitability, there is often confusion about how to do the job well.

It's time now to take out the family photo album, to talk to our grandmothers – and our great-grandmothers, if we have them. We need to access our own history, and take our place in the mother-line, for the sake of our daughters and our daughters' daughters.

Further Reading

Aria, Barbara *Mamatoto: A Celebration of Birth* (Virago Press, London, 1991)

Balaskas, Janet *Natural Pregnancy: A Practical, Holistic Guide to Wellbeing from Conception to Birth* (Gaia Books, London and Interlink Publishing Group, New York, 1990)

Blanks, Tim (ed.) *The Body Shop Book* (Little, Brown & Co., London, 1994)

Campion, Kitty *Holistic Herbal for Mother and Baby* (Bloomsbury Publishing, London, 1996)

Crystal, David *Listen to Your Child: A Parent's Guide to Children's Language* (Penguin Books, London and New York, 1986)

Culpeper, Nicholas *Culpeper's Book of Birth*, Ian Thomas (ed.) (Webb & Bower, Exeter, Devon, 1985)

Gavin, Jamila *Our Favourite Stories* (Dorling Kindersley, London and New York, 1997)

Hessing, Perle *A Mirror to My Life* (Cameron Books, London, 1987)

Hoffman, Mary and Ray, Jane *Song of the Earth* (Orion Books, London, 1995)

Husain, S. *The Goddess* (Macmillan, London and Little, Brown & Co., Boston, 1997)

Jackson, A. J. *Eye Signs* (Thorsons, London, 1995)

Jackson, Deborah *Baby Wisdom: The World's Best Secrets for the First Year of Parenting* (Hodder and Stoughton, London, 2002)

Jackson, Deborah *Letting Go as Children Grow* (Bloomsbury Publishing, London and New York, 2003)

Jackson, Deborah *Three in a Bed* (Bloomsbury Publishing, London and New York, 2003)

Kindersley, Anabel and Barnabas *Children Just Like Me: Celebrations* (Dorling Kindersley, London and New York, 1995)

Kitzinger, Sheila *The Crying Baby* (Penguin Books, London and New York, 1990)

Kitzinger, Sheila (ed.) *The Midwife Challenge* (Pandora Press, Ontario, 1988)

La Leche League *The Womanly Art of Breastfeeding* (Penguin Books, London and New York, 1997)

Marks, Anthony and Tingay, Graham *The Romans* (Usborne Publishing, London and EDC Publications, San José, 1990)

Montagu, Ashley *Touching: The Human Significance of the Skin* (HarperCollins Publishers, London and New York, 1986)

Morris, Desmond *Babywatching* (Ebury Press, London, 1995)

Pilling, Ann *Creation: Stories From Around the World* (Walker Books, London, 1997)

Priya, Jacqeline Vincent *Birth Traditions & Modern Pregnancy Care* (Element, Shaftesbury, Dorset, 1992)

Rudd, Carol *Flower Essences* (Element, Shaftesbury, Dorset and Penguin, New York, 1998)

Stewart, R. J. *Celtic Gods, Celtic Goddesses* (Blandford Press,London, 1992)

Sutherland, Anne (ed.) *Face Values* (BBC Books, London,1978)

Taylor, Colin *North American Indians* (Parragon Books, Bristol, 1997)

Willes, Margaret *Memories of Childhood* (The National Trust, London, 1997)

Index